TRUST ME

ALSO BY JOSEPH MYERS

The Search to Belong

Organic Community

ALSO BY KEVIN BAIRD

Whole

TRUST ME

discovering trust in a culture of distrust

Joseph R. Myers
with
Kevin Baird and Dr. Jesus Jara

Copyright © 2023 by Joseph Myers

Published by

Meteor Education Publishing (MEpub)

All rights reserved. No part of this publication may be reproduced, distributed, or transmitted in any form or by any means, including photocopying, recording, or other electronic or mechanical methods, without the prior written permission of the publisher, except in the case of brief quotations embodied in critical reviews and certain other noncommercial uses permitted by copyright law. For permission requests, write to the publisher, addressed "Attention: Publisher," at the address below.

Meteor Education Publishing

690 NE 23rd Ave, Gainesville, FL 32609

meteoreducationpublishing.com

MEpub / Meteor Education Publishing is a division or Meteor Education. The name and logo are trademarks of Meteor Education.

Published in association with the literary agency of Mark Oestreicher.

The publisher is not responsible for websites (or their content) that are not owned by the publisher. Readers should be aware that Internet Web sites offered as citations and/or sources for further information may have changed or disappeared between the time this was written and when it is read.

Some names and identifying details have been changed to protect the privacy of individuals. Stories within may sound like your story and probably are yours and hundreds of others.

Cover and internal design: Joseph R. Myers

Illustrations: Michael Lagocki

ISBN

Paperback: 978-1-7334334-8-8   E-Book: 978-1-7334334-9-5

Printed in the United States of America

THIS BOOK IS DEDICATED TO:

Gail Hamilton
who exhibited healthy distrust and healthy trust

Praise for Trust Me:

Diving right in with a story from his own life to illustrate the key concept that we can trust and distrust at the same time, Joseph Myers takes on a deep dive into one of the most important topics of our time. **Trust Me** *is thoughtful, well-researched and readable as it explores how trust and distrust operate in our lives, and how to build, strengthen, and maintain it in the relationships that matter to us. I highly recommend* **Trust Me** *as a great addition to the growing list of must-read books on this subject.*

— Charles Feltman, author The Thin Book of Trust 2nd edition

Trust Me *is an indispensable guide for anyone seeking to cultivate trust within teams. With his remarkable ability to translate cutting-edge brain science into actionable strategies, Myers presents a captivating and practical toolkit that has become my go-to resource. Whether you're looking to build trust from scratch or mend fractured relationships, this book equips you with the essential insights and techniques necessary for success.*

—Rex Miller, renowned expert in optimizing human and team performance, strategic foresight, and organizational transformation. Five-time, International award winning Wiley Author, author.

"Trust is the essential base layer for all relationships, whether in the workplace or beyond. **Trust Me** is an essential, practical guide for understanding the nature of trust (and distrust), and more importantly how to build deep, trustworthy connections with others and yourself."

—Todd Henry, Author of Herding Tigers

"Joseph Myers has a knack for turning a subject inside out like a sock, and then knocking our socks off with his original takes, aired-out perspectives and brilliant brainstorms. **Trust Me** takes arguably the #1 issue of our time, trust, and revolutionizes how we look at it and live by it."

—Leonard Sweet, best-selling author, professor, publisher, podcaster and chief contributor to PreachTheStory.com

Trust Me takes on the timely topic of trust and turns our conventional thinking upside down. This book breaks down our personal role in developing individual and collective trust and explores the intricacies of the trust continuum. Taking a proactive and understanding approach, readers can apprehend the nuances of trust/distrust and ways to build a trusting culture and connection.

—LindaGail Walker, author of Surviving the Storm: Leading through Post-Traumatic Growth

"I've been a part of and built teams for years – trust always comes up as the foundation of a strong team, and while everyone agrees with that, the actual steps to understand trust and distrust, measure, and continually build trust throughout the duration of the time together eludes even the highest performing teams – until now. **Trust Me** *takes the complexities of trust and presents them in a way that can be understood and applied by all, truly making trust an intentional effort. From the flywheel to his practical way to measure trust to the relational stages, Joseph breaks the mystical nature of trust and gives team members a path to follow to truly understand, build, and reinforce trust."*

—Kyle Majchrowski Founder, Ripple Intent

Myers' work has been shaping my thinking and work for decades, and the insights of **Trust Me** *have already seeped into my coaching work, my speaking engagements, even conversations with my spouse. It's not an exaggeration to write that I am discovering implications of these truths in every aspect of my life. Sure, educators will benefit from this work; but that's mostly because they are human beings--and all humans, at least those who want to grow in self-knowledge and proactive trust-building, will benefit from these ideas.*

—Mark Oestreicher, author, founder/partner in The Youth Cartel

For additional information and resources scan the QR code above

Trust Me

Thank You

A work that develops over decades has many contributors: those who knowingly and unknowingly found their way into the fabric of this book. It would be impossible to thank each one, yet each one brought insight, wisdom, artifacts, and the magic of Trust and Distrust.

We thank our families and friends who put up with the undying pursuit to collect the pieces of this puzzle. We thank our coworkers and colleagues for their patience and encouragement. We thank all the strangers who unknowingly allowed us to watch how they journeyed through Trust and Distrust. To all our most profound thanks!

To the extraordinary people who worked tirelessly to make this work into a book: Johno, Ainsley, Jennifer, and Marko, we thank you for your amazing belief and labor. Bill and the Meteor family, thank you for your faith and for cheerleading this work forward.

Preface

As a business owner serving the educational K-12 textbook and teacher resource market, trust has always been at the forefront of my mind. Trust is a fundamental aspect of any successful business, and building and maintaining trust is essential in the world of education. However, my journey has led me to question and challenge common assumptions about trust and distrust, particularly in the wake of a personal experience that shattered trust in my own life.

In this book, I share my observations and insights into the complex nature of trust and distrust. It all started with a realization that trust and distrust are not two sides of the same coin but rather separate entities that operate independently and react to different stimuli. I discovered that trust is processed in the prefrontal cortex of the brain, where complex decision-making occurs, while distrust is processed in the amygdala, the primitive part responsible for our fight-or-flight response. Simply, we decide to trust, and we feel distrust.

Through research and personal observations, I came to understand that trust and distrust have distinctive languages, motivators, and triggers. Factors such as gender, personality type, past trauma, and demographic backgrounds further shape our interpretations and responses to trust and distrust. It became clear that trust is a dynamic force, begetting trustworthiness and driving positive relationships, while the absence of trust leads to apathy and erodes the foundations of interactions and transactions.

In today's world, characterized by rapid technological advancements and a shifting cultural landscape, the concept of trust is more crucial than ever. Trust in traditional institutions has been shaken, and we find ourselves grappling with a perceived "trust crisis." However, amidst the uncertainty and contradictions, trust remains a cornerstone for building healthy and productive relationships. Understanding the dynamics of trust and learning to navigate the complexities of trust and distrust interactions is vital.

Throughout this book, we will explore the multifaceted nature of trust and its far-reaching impact in various domains. From personal relationships to business success, trust plays a central role in achieving our goals. We will delve into the Trust Flywheel, a tool for intentionally building and maintaining trust, and examine the detrimental effects of a lack of trust. By redefining trust's relationship with distrust, we gain a fresh perspective on this powerful force and its potential to transform our lives and society.

This book aims to provide insights and practical guidance for individuals seeking to cultivate trust, both personally and professionally. By understanding the intricate workings of trust and learning how to navigate the complexities of trust and distrust, we can forge meaningful connections, foster growth, and thrive in a world that relies on trust more than ever before.

So, join me on this journey as we unravel the mysteries of trust and discover how it can shape our lives, relationships, and the world around us.

Joseph R. Myers

Kevin Baird and Dr. Jesus Jara kindly contributed their insights, wisdom, and experience throughout the book. In addition, at the end of each chapter you'll find the Guide Dog symbol indicating their direct writing.

Contents

Preface VII

INTRO: TRUST ME: YOU CAN'T TRUST ME
    How the Brain Processes Trust and Distrust 1

1: TRUST ME: IT'S NOT JUST IN YOUR HEAD
    No One Trusts Any Longer 15

2: TRUST ME: IT'S A DOGFIGHT
    The Personalities of Distrust 27

3: TRUST ME: SIZE MATTERS
    Measuring Trust 47

4: TRUST ME: IT'S ALL ABOUT MOMENTUM
    The Trust Flywheel 63

5: TRUST ME: I LET YOU DOWN
    Dealing With Broken Trust 85

6: TRUST ME: IT'S YOU
    Developing Strong Self-Trust 109

7: TRUST ME: WE'RE IN THIS TOGETHER
    Building a Culture of Trust 121

Appendix 144

Endnotes 147

Discovering Trust in a Culture of Distrust

Trust Me:
You Can't Trust Me!

How the Brain Processes Trust and Distrust

Trust me, there have been seasons in my life where the last thing you'd want to do is trust me.

In the mid-1980s during heated conversations with my now ex-wife, she would exclaim, "How can I ever trust you again!?... You've broken my trust...I can't trust you with anything!" The conversation would go on for several minutes and then end in tears. "How can I stay with someone I can't trust? It will take years, or maybe never, for me to trust you again."

She was right. I had severely broken her trust, and it would be "never" before she would trust me again. However, it was because of this "never" that what happened next confused and intrigued me:

In the midst of distrust's debilitating pain, my ex nonetheless handed me her most prized possession: a little girl clutching a pink, child-sized My Little Pony suitcase, **our daughter**.

How could she vow to never again believe anything I ever said and yet still have confidence in me with our daughter? Can high levels of trust and distrust exist at the same time?

These thoughts were counter to the way I'd learned that trust worked. Yet as I continued to watch and experience how this worked in real life, I couldn't help but question common "truths" of trust. Statements like, "It takes time to rebuild trust once broken" seemed unlikely when an action of trust would immediately follow. "I can't trust you with anything" was increasingly confusing as I witnessed a trust leap in the next encounter.

My tragic divorce altered my life's path in many significant ways. It changed the way I observed the world and those around me. I began gaining new insights into how people belong and build community, how organic systems are sometimes altered into fabricated institutional systems, and how observing people, with as little bias as possible, leads to unconventional understandings of the natural universe.[1] The system of trust and distrust is no different. Separating trust from distrust was the first disruptive observation and has (so far) taken the longest to develop and understand.

TRUST AND DISTRUST ARE SEPARATE ENTITIES

At first, it seemed absurd to consider trust and distrust as two separate, unattached entities. I understood trust and distrust as opposite ends of one spectrum, or balancing on a scale. It seemed obvious that if you have more of one, you would have less of the other. But the more I let myself observe people's actions, free of mainstream presuppositions, the more it became clear: trust and distrust operate independently, react to different stimuli, and speak different languages.

However, beyond my personal observations, the existing research consistently married trust and distrust as two sides of the same coin. Until recently, there wasn't "hard evidence" that these two concepts should be considered as detached and studied individually. The more I researched, the crazier I felt. I took long breaks from reading the experts to observe people in everyday situations. These anecdotal observations continued to confirm my theory that trust and distrust are experienced and implemented separately.

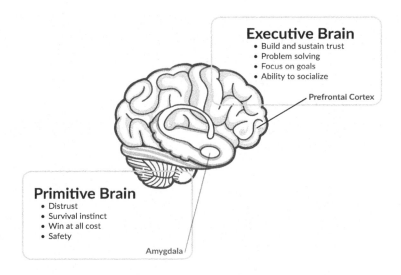

Over the last few years, significant discoveries have advanced the mainstream understanding about how the brain processes our emotions, decisions, and actions. Scientists have discovered the brain processes trust and distrust from two separate zones. Trust is processed in the prefrontal cortex, while distrust is processed in the amygdala.

Both of these areas have significantly different purposes. The prefrontal cortex is where the mind makes decisions based on complex logical thought. It's where we assemble the puzzle pieces of life into an order that generates a path or conclusion ending in a relationship. The amygdala, on the other hand, is the primitive, fight-flight-or-freeze response part of our brain. It processes feelings instinctively. It is the "Guard Dog" of our mind—more on that in Chapter 2.

These two regions of the brain process our reactions to the world differently. They are motivated to action by different incentives and have distinctive native languages. For example, the amygdala responds in nanoseconds to the facial features of an oncoming stranger to determine whether or not to distrust.

By contrast, the prefrontal cortex takes its time to engage, while it curates a list of reasons one might begin to trust. The prefrontal cortex responds to trust symbols like a uniform or a religious icon, while the amygdala "hears" warning signals, alerting us to what the amygdala views as high-risk traits, such as covering up with a hoodie in broad daylight or standing too close for comfort. We must point out, and will discuss further later, that sometimes our amygdala decides to warn us about something that is not actually a danger because of a previous unsafe or undesirable experience.

In addition to trust and distrust operating in different parts of the brain, gender, personality type, past trauma, generation, race, wealth status, and other demographic factors nuance how we interpret, feel, and respond. Men and women trust and distrust differently. Thus, when trust is broken and in need of repair, each gender looks for different iconography for restoration. Similarly, different personalities respond to triggers of trust and distrust according to their type. Someone who grew up in the city looks for different markers of trustworthiness than someone who grew up in a rural area, and on and on. We'll talk more about those differences in Chapter 5.

A COMPLEX TRUST CRISIS?

Maybe more than ever we are confronted with complex situations that require both trust and distrust. In conjunction with rapidly accelerating technologies, over the last hundred years in the West we have seen tectonic cultural shifts, blurring our trust in traditionally trustworthy institutions. Headline-makers and their advertisers cultivate our feelings of distrust and make money off of the fear that accompanies it. News outlets, thought leaders, and researchers have crescendoed their diagnosis: we are living through a "trust crisis." Over the decades, the U.S. has been shaken by national financial meltdowns and betrayed by representatives we elected, religious leaders who are corrupt or impotent in the face of crisis, and increasing misinformation and manipulation from the Fourth Estate.[2] As we observe trust and distrust interactions processed in the exploding digital world, we find ourselves cartographers armed with paper maps for a flat earth.

Who can we trust? When we believe we can only choose to trust or distrust, our fear is that we can trust no one. If trust and distrust are two ends of the same spectrum, then obviously we can only distrust our environment and the people around us in this time of crisis. This prospect is frightening and exhausting, especially because we instinctively want to trust and have trusting relationships we can rely on! When we trust a person or organization and they let us down, it makes us think we are a bad judge of character - which can make us feel unsafe with our own judgments. (Making space for our own healthy distrust, at the same time as we are choosing to build trust in a relationship, is an essential skill we'll talk about in Chapter 6.)

At the core of all this we wonder, "Can it be fixed?" Can we ever trust a president again? Will the media regain the trusted "Cronkite" status they once enjoyed? Can we trust our financial future to banks and Wall Street? Can we ever rely on a spiritual leader or group to care for us and have the answers we need?

In spite of how you may be feeling after reading all that, the answer to these questions is a resounding "Yes!" Trust is stronger than ever. As I observe individuals going about their daily lives, I witness an abundance of trust. We are trusting and trustworthy. We might distrust institutions and organizations more than our grandparents and great-grandparents, but we haven't given up on trusting individuals, even strangers, with life's everyday goings-on. The more we understand that our brains actually trust and distrust at the same time, the more we'll be able to navigate the current "trust crisis."

> "Why? Because without trust, and without an understanding of how it is built, managed, lost, and repaired, a society cannot survive, and it certainly cannot thrive. Trust is fundamental to almost every action, relationship and transaction. The emerging trust shift isn't simply the story of a dizzying upsurge in technology or the rise of new business models. It's a social and cultural revolution. It's about us. And it matters." [3]

The more we learn about trust, the more we may become convinced it is a magical remedy that can heal everything from interpersonal relationships to world economies. In almost every field of study, trust is one of the key lubricants for success.

If you want to create a good family, raise great children, or get along with your in-laws, trust is the foundational element. It stands above love, compassion, safety, and provision. If you want to build a successful business, trust is the cornerstone you will need. Want an economic system with sustainable growth? You guessed it, trust is an essential component. Do you want to become a great leader? More than any other factor, obtaining people's trust will not only let you achieve your goal, but will allow you to remain their leader through thick and thin.

TRUST IS DYNAMIC

As we will unravel later, trust begets trust, which begets trustworthiness. This equation is society's most valuable power plant. In Chapter 4, we will study the Trust Flywheel, a tool for intentionally engaging the process of developing trust in relationships. Trust momentum needs to be continually fed by this process, and that momentum helps in healing broken trust, and strengthening trust over time. A parent, political candidate, teacher, or leader who exhibits that they can trust will in turn be trusted, and that process brands them trustworthy. In every connection, from personal to institutional to societal, trust is the key indicator and predictor of health.

Conversely, the lack of trust is devastating. A deficiency in trust nourishes apathy. The lack of trust not only inhibits success, but an ever-increasing distrust erodes the underpinnings of transactions and interactions and leaves relationships void of "relations." Peer into any fragmented home, marriage, government, or world system and you'll find the absence of trust and an increasing presence of distrust.

Trust is a hot topic globally as historically reliable institutions of trust are increasingly not trustworthy.

> "Like the plot of some overblown soap opera or Jacobean tragedy, the episodes of unethical behaviour have come thick and fast, from the lurid, even criminal, to the just plain stupid and, sadly, routine. Each has chipped away at public confidence. The British MPs' expenses scandal; the false intelligence about weapons of mass destruction (WMDs); Tesco's horsemeat outrage; price gouging by big pharma; the BP Deepwater Horizon oil spill; the dishonours of FIFA's bribery; Volkswagen's 'dieselgate'; major data breaches from companies such as Sony, Yahoo! and Target;

> the Panama Papers and widespread tax avoidance; the exchange-rate manipulation by the world's largest banks ; Brazil's Petrobras oil scandal ; the lack of an effective response to the refugee crises; and , last but not least , shocking revelations of widespread abuse by Catholic priests , other clergy and other ' care ' institutions . No wonder a thousand headlines lament that nobody trusts authority any more. Corruption, elitism, economic disparity-and the feeble responses to all of the above-have pummeled traditional trust in the old institutions as fiercely as a brutal wind lashing ancient oaks." [4]

We're seemingly surrounded by overwhelming evidence that the world and those in it cannot be trusted. A "trust crisis"? Quite possibly. Are trust behaviors and historic trust centers fluctuating? No question. And in the midst of all this uncertainty and contradiction, trust remains an essential building block for every relationship. Defining trust and distrust, then, becomes not only the goal of this book, but the goal for anyone pursuing healthy and productive relationships.

A RELATIONSHIP WITH THE UNKNOWN

Until now, the tools available to us have made defining trust as challenging as walking through a minefield. Each "exploding" definition exposes only the part of the field it's "protecting." The good news: it's all within a tiny field. Whether in sociology, economics, education, relationships, or any other field of study, more research has been conducted on the subject of trust than the examination of any other relational component. Confidence, reliability, contract of hoped guarantees, a conduit, a lubricant, and yearned expectations all are words (or concepts) that have made their way into definitions of trust.

Rachel Botsman's simple definition is helpful and precise. *"Trust is a confident relationship with the unknown."*[5]

Obviously, trust is a multifaceted notion. It doesn't have a single definition that works for all situations. Much like love, trust is something people apparently "know when they see (experience) it." It's gooey. Yet, it has more substance and influence than any other relational component.

There are many good resources you can use to dive deeper into the definition of trust. While trust is one of the topics of this book, the relationship between trust and distrust is the distinguishing theme. So, what about distrust? What is the definition of distrust? We now know it's not simply the opposite of trust.

So how should we define it?

Distrust is distinctly different from the "opposite of trust." The opposite of trust is the lack or absence of trust. Trust's opposite is low trust: the lack of confidence, reliability, contract of hoped guarantees... you get the idea, and that is not the same as distrust. You can lack confidence in someone without distrusting them. And you can distrust someone personally, but trust them to uphold a business contract. As we mentioned, trust and distrust are detached. They are not different sides of the same coin. The mind processes them from different areas of the brain. Therefore, they have different motivators, languages, triggers, and purposes. Therefore, we can experience both at the same time, toward the same person, scenario, or institution.

TRUST: REDEFINED

As noted earlier, trust is processed in the prefrontal cortex of the brain. The prefrontal cortex is responsible for rational (and sometimes not so rational) calculated thoughts. The prefrontal cortex is the forward part of the frontal lobe. It's behind your eyes and forehead. This brain region is occupied with planning complex cognitive behavior, expressing personality, making decisions, and moderating social behavior. It is the great conductor of the orchestra of the mind. It takes what it receives from the rest of the brain and decides how to act, react, and differentiate between dissonant thoughts.

Distrust, on the other hand, is processed in the amygdala. This primitive area influences both left and right hemispheres of the brain, and responds to important, or seemingly important, environmental stimuli. For example, in dangerous situations, the amygdala kicks into action and encourages our fight-or-flight response. "If the amygdala perceives a correspondence between the record of experiences in the hippocampus and incoming information, and judges that the stimulus warrants a fight, flight, or freeze response, then it will trigger the hypothalamic—pituitary—adrenal (HPA) axis and 'hijack' the prefrontal cortex (PFC), partly in the form of blood flow being redirected from the PFC to the limbic system."[6] The amygdala is the "first responder" of our brain and is in control of our "early warning system" when a quick protective reaction is needed.

What do we learn from this exploration of how the brain works?

SIMPLY, WE DECIDE TO TRUST, AND WE FEEL DISTRUST.

One of the technologies that can help us understand and feel confident (and less confused!) about how we experience trust and distrust is a system for measuring. In Chapter 3, we dive into the three containers we use to measure trust. Identifying each and knowing why we measure with this framework reduces confusion and helps us identify how to develop trust in each container.

Trust and distrust, then, are not opposites. In fact, they can be allies: they can work in harmony to secure trustworthiness. They are very independent and sometimes fight. They can both be dominant and both be submissive. However, when working for the same healthy goal together, they are our best tools for secure, productive, fulfilling relationships. Thus, I will add to Rachel Botsman's excellent definition:

Trust is a confident relationship with the unknown, and a guiding distrust of the known.

THE CURRENCY OF INTERACTIONS

There's nothing that compares with the destructive nature of broken trust within society, organizations, and relationships. Encouragingly, there's nothing that equals the strength of the bonds between us when we do trust each other. Trust is our most fragile and most precious asset. The more we trust, the more empathetic we are with one another, and the more we trust, the more trustworthy we become to those around us. Trust is a powerful societal glue. It builds the roads to stronger societies, better organizations, and richer relationships. "Money may be the currency of transactions, but trust is the currency of interactions."[7] There may be no better way to express our humanity than this.

However, we should not be naive when we decide to trust. How can we trust with confidence? The answer is found as we separate the roles of trust and distrust. Healthy distrust offers a safe starting point, and provides the Trust Flywheel with the friction needed to make a strong decision to trust. We must understand that distrust is a necessary ally to trust. We cannot safely trust without healthy distrust. The goal is not to eliminate all distrust. Instead, our goal is to move distrust from a reactive "Guard Dog" to a well-trained "Guide Dog."

As we traverse the next seven chapters, we begin to reframe our language. "I don't trust you!" doesn't equal "I distrust you." Likewise, "I trust you" doesn't mean that I have little or no distrust in you. I've painstakingly tried to be precise and break the limiting chains of this kind of language. It is important to separate the two because doing so gives us the power to heal and repair relationships that have been severed by broken trust.

If our only option lies within a single spectrum of trust to distrust, we are held hostage by the emotions of our amygdala or the calculated process of the prefrontal cortex: one constantly pushing the other out to take dominance. Having the freedom to hold a high level of distrust while deciding to trust again gives us the

authority and control to heal and sustain trust relationships. Trust and distrust are not at war. They are allies. Together they take us by each hand and walk us into a healthy and hopeful culture of trust.

Trust and distrust are essential for every interaction, every connection, and every transaction. It's crucial we develop a complete understanding of how trust and distrust are developed, repaired, and sustained. **Trust Me** re-imagines how trust and distrust collaborate to protect, enhance, and stabilize our lives...together.

Our mission is to inspire a genuine shift in how educators perceive and engage with the educational environment. This book uncovers a vital but often overlooked aspect of this environment—one that remains hidden from plain sight. You may not witness it unfolding in real-time, yet its impact is undeniably real. It pulsates through the fabric of education, and that force is trust. Trust represents the result of intricate biological processes occurring within two regions of the brain: the amygdala and the prefrontal cortex.

*Let's face it: educators are incredibly busy. Heck, the whole world seems to be in a perpetual rush these days. When was the last time you actually had the time to read an entire book, cover to cover? It's been a while, hasn't it? We get it. That's why this book takes a different approach. We want to make things easier for educators. You can quickly scan through and see if any eye-catching headers resonate with you. But we don't stop there. We give you clear directions—this is what to do—and break down the implications—this is what it means—for your school. **Trust Me** is designed to be super easy to grasp, highly practical, and incredibly useful in your everyday teaching journey.*

Trust Me:
It's Not Just In Your Head

No One Trusts Any Longer

"Distrust is defined as: what I shared with you, is not safe with you."
—Bren'e Brown[8]

Trust me, your mom was right. You shouldn't trust strangers.

Or she was at least kind of right.

By the mid 1980s, the United States radiated power. The economic and political recovery from the late '70s made President Reagan a trusted American hero. His Hollywood cowboy demeanor instilled confidence and united much of the nation. He brought back the hostages and beat back the effects of high interest rates, and the U. S. was once again a superpower on the world stage. Even in a time when most people were in a high alert, high distrust state, Reagan found a way to end the Cold War. He mitigated distrust in order to build trust.

In the '80s the nation's greatest fears were nuclear. Our nemesis, Russia, spent years stockpiling hidden nuclear warheads and President Reagan made this threat his focus. We had been told we'd need treaties that limited nuclear weapons to bring peace to the world. For a time, the arrogant posturing of two superpowers' attempts to meet in the middle provided kindling for headlines and late-night talk shows.

At a critical moment, President Reagan sought and received wise counsel. Suzanne Massie reminded the president that Russians like to talk in proverbs. She taught him the iconic Reaganism that is forever woven into American culture:

Trust, but verify.

The Intermediate-Range Nuclear Forces Treaty (INF) was successfully signed by General Secretary Mikhail Gorbachev and President Ronald Reagan on December 8, 1987. It was a better answer to nuclear weapons. For the first time in history, the treaty eliminated an entire class of U.S. and Soviet missiles. "It's a good bargain. For every nuclear warhead of our own that we remove, they will give up four."[9]

"Trust, but verify" worked...The agreement felt like a "safer world." And Gorbachev wasn't the only one convinced by the short proverb. Reagan's genius was that he allowed the American public, and the world, to listen in on his conversation with Gorbachev. If the president proclaimed our nation should only trust our enemy, and not distrust, he would not have gained the significant support needed to make a treaty with Russia. Coming out of the intense, constant, frightening messaging of the Cold War, Reagan acknowledged that U.S. citizens had reasons to be distrustful. Rather than just expecting citizens to trust him when he went to negotiate with "the enemy," he kept the negotiations public and open to scrutiny. The invitation to distrust opened a pathway for citizens to begin to feel safe trusting Reagan's plan and Russia's agreements.

"Trust, but verify" is allowing distrust to guide the decision to trust. It is trust and distrust working as allies. This tactic lowered the anxiety of a nation. Giving Americans permission to distrust while trusting allowed them to see Reagan as a trustworthy president. It lowered the angst of deciding to trust, especially when the risks were high.

Most often the word distrust carries a negative overtone. However, distrust is an essential component of relational health. And lucky for us, we distrust a good number of things. It is a collaborator with trust and an essential part of the trust process.

Unfortunately for our Western obsession with progress, the U.S. hasn't become an increasingly healthy trust culture since Reagan's big win. We have experienced catastrophes in every area of life over the last 40 years that have amplified our distrust and encouraged horrible habits that erode our trust relationships. Don't worry: in the end, a brief study of the current trust landscape in the U.S. will support our efforts to nurture healthy distrust and healthy trust in ourselves and others. It's not a permanent state of things that:

TRUST IS DEAD

"(W)e have to trust to survive. Paradoxically, we have to lie to survive as well." [10]

"You can't trust anyone anymore" is the dramatic undertone of daily headlines.

It may be truer than we are willing to admit. "According to studies by several researchers, most of us encounter nearly two hundred lies a day. That means if you're lucky enough to get eight hours of sleep a night, you've likely been on the receiving end of about twelve lies an hour."[11] You would think this would make us more skeptical of each other (and subconsciously it has), but ironically all this lying is focused on one outcome: more trust! How so?

We lie to urge others to trust us and we do it in a couple of different ways. Sometimes we lie to make ourselves look good. Other times we lie to make others feel good about us. Sometimes we appeal to the prefrontal cortex with discussion and reason, to encourage others to decide to trust. And sometimes we attempt to soothe the amygdala when lying by our mannerisms or tone, hoping others feel less distrust. We will nuance this significant difference more in Chapter 5; however, no matter the path, the motivation is the same. Humans crave, need, and expect others to trust, and we're often willing to lie to ensure they do.

Maybe we should revise Mom's advice: it's not just strangers who pose a threat...don't trust anyone!

The grim statistics don't stop with our compulsive lying to family, friends, and neighbors. Year after year, the amount of trust U.S. citizens place in government, business, media, and other organizations falls. Fewer than 47% of Americans trust the media, which is understandable as the Fourth Estate has been proven time and again to be lying to us to please their advertisers. More than 62% of the U.S. population distrust their CEOs' messages and decisions. [12]

What about a historic staple of trust, the church? While the church and religious organizations are still among the most trusted institutions,[13] their leaders have taken a hard hit. Religious leaders don't fare much better than business CEOs. We used to trust the church and its leaders to take care of us from birth to death, but we've shifted that trust to alternatives. Furthermore, the way religious leaders have mishandled (and been part of) scandals, made selfish financial decisions, provided simple answers to complex problems, and generally demonstrated a lack of integrity make us even more distrustful of them. In fact, most citizens trust the military and science significantly more than leaders in religious organizations.[14]

Over the last hundred years, we can observe U.S. public trust shifting from church and the traditional family unit to education and business. Unfortunately, capitalism has failed to reward younger generations as it previously rewarded people with degrees and long-term job commitments in the years following World War II. As the poverty and wealthy classes in the US expand and the middle class shrinks, we have become more polarized in our politics and more suspicious of our media. People have rallied around our supposedly representative government. However, we are gradually realizing our representatives and journalists are more likely to be loyal to their donors than to their constituents, and again, large buckets of public trust have shifted to one of the final reliable Western institutions: the medical and scientific community.

Sadly, in conjunction with being betrayed and manipulated by our news institutions over the last few decades, more and more evidence is emerging that our medical institutions lie to us as well. This lack of safety "at home" has led more and more U.S. citizens to lash out at other countries, as if they're the problem—leading to heightened trust in the military industrial complex to protect us. This reaction is similar to a child being abused at home and turning into a bully of his peers at school.

What's going on? It might be easy to conclude, given the evidence, that trust is dead in the United States. However, trust is very much alive and well—it's just showing up in new ways.

TRUST IS (NOT!) DEAD, BUT ITS CENTERS ARE SHIFTING

Good news: trust is not dead! But the world has changed, and the objects of our trust, the centers we traditionally put our trust in, have changed, too. Dramatically.

You know how your parents trust your family doctor's word more than you do, and your grandparents trust the doctors even more? Are you likely to verify a diagnosis online even if you trust the doctor is giving you good advice? Generationally we have shifted the who and what that we trust. This is important. Trust hasn't gone anywhere... it's just moving around. We are moving away from the institutions and toward something else. You can think of it as a shift from vertical trust to horizontal trust.

Institutional Trust is Shifting to Distributed Trust

Consider these statistics from Rachel Botsman's study on technology:

> "(W)e can see that trust falls into distinct chapters. The first was local, when we lived within the boundaries of small local communities where everyone knew everyone else. The second was institutional, a kind of intermediated trust that ran through a variety of contracts, courts and corporate brands, freeing commerce from local exchanges and creating the foundation necessary for an organized industrial society. And the third, still very much in its infancy, is distributed. A trust shift need not mean the previous forms will be completely superseded; only that the new form will become more dominant...Trust that used to flow upwards to referees and regulators, to authorities and experts, to watchdogs and gatekeepers, is now flowing horizontally, in some instances to our fellow human beings and, in other cases, to (computer) programs and bots. Trust is being turned on its head. The old sources of power, expertise and authority no longer hold all the aces, or even the deck of cards. The consequences of that, good and bad, cannot be underestimated."[15]

Examining our past trust systems provides insight into why our culture currently triggers our amygdala to distrust so readily. It also provides clues for moving forward, since humans have participated in something similar to distributed trust in the past, when we trusted based on who was in our local community.

Institutional trust orients around power centers, often authority figures, we are culturally predisposed to trust ("everyone around me trusts them..."). Our social and personal familiarity with power centers makes the trust process a lot faster than when we encounter an authority figure or seek help from an institution that we have no familiarity or cultural history with. For example, in the U.S. we generally expect to go out and find our own romantic partner, but in countries like Japan, Korea, China, the Netherlands, Russia, India, and Thailand, the role of matchmaker is a power center people trust to guide and even make their partnership decisions.[16,17] All over the world, different cultures rely on their own power centers to shorten the sometimes arduous process of trusting so their daily lives flow more easily.

For people who grew up experiencing and enjoying the benefits of the institutional trust style, risk emerges when a power center shifts suddenly and the Guard Dog Distrust (Chapter 2) is commanded into action. To many U.S. citizens, police officers are a culturally accepted and reliable center of institutional trust. Police, as an institution, are expected to uphold law and order, and by doing so, help keep society safe and fair. Police are a significant institutional trust power center—until they are not. This dissonance is part of the widespread tensions we are negotiating culturally right now. It is especially impactful when a formerly trusted person or institution is shown to be untrustworthy, because when we feel unexpectedly unsafe, we realize we were vulnerable, and when we feel vulnerable we tend to become defensively angry. The longer an individual has experienced institutional trust as a reliable way of being, the more likely they are to feel destabilized, defensive, and distrusting of the rapidly evolving distributed trust behaviors.

Distributed trust is when trust in power centers is dissolved in favor of trust power nodes across entire networks webbing throughout society. Now that historic mainstream institutions are proving increasingly untrustworthy, and we have expansive access to communications and research technology, we are not always putting all our trust eggs in a few baskets! Instead, individuals and their various tribes decide who's trustworthy and who is not, and trust shifts quickly if the object proves untrustworthy.[18] In a real sense it's "Power to the People."

Distrust's sole purpose is to guide us to safety. Trust's primary goal is building relational capital.

As we keep discovering, we are in a time of rapid change and exponential evolution. It is important to bear in mind that, depending on age and other demographics, you, your loved ones, and your colleagues are all experiencing different imprints and priorities about how you prefer to trust. To those of us who are more comfortable with institutional trust, distributed trust feels gooey and foggy, like walking on quicksand. And this is prime real estate for distrust to germinate. We feel safer knowing there are just a few power centers in our environment, knowing who is in charge, and knowing who to blame when something goes wrong. Those of us who are aware that we've been betrayed by historic power centers of trust feel more comfortable with distributed trust. We feel safer knowing that if one power node of our trust network fails us, we are still supported by plenty of other trust nodes.

So trust is not dead—but it is in transition. The world's infrastructure has changed. Cultural, sociological, and financial "tectonic plates" have shifted, and we distrust the ground we walked on so firmly before the quake. Therefore:

Distrust is playing a more prominent role as we experience trust shifting. Maybe we should reword Reagan's proverb: Distrust, but verify!

SO WHAT IS DISTRUST?

Distrust is NOT the opposite of trust. Distrust is its own concept, and although connected to trust, it operates independently. Distrust is autonomous. Low trust or lack of trust are not the same as distrust. Distrust has its own purpose, language, goal, and process independent from trust. Distrust's sole purpose is to guide us to safety. Trust's primary goal is building relational capital. Healthy distrust builds a wall of safety and provides a sanctuary from which to make a strong decision to trust.

RECOGNIZING THE DIFFERENCE: LOW TRUST vs DISTRUST

When a low level of trust AND a low level of distrust are present, the outcome is apathy. Distrust never expresses, "I don't care!" Only low trust and low distrust together result in this type of apathetic response.

Protection, aggression, and guidance are not activated by low levels of trust. These reactions are only engaged when we experience distrust. If any active defensive emotion is experienced, it's a result of distrust. When we say, "I don't trust you," we're often saying, "I distrust you."

It's important to recognize when and at what level distrust is present.

Low trust, on the other hand, is characterized by a general lack of confidence. You don't distrust that person or organization, you don't feel afraid of them—you just don't know enough about them to begin trusting them for any reason. To help discern the difference between distrust and low trust, keep an eye out for defensive feelings or detached feelings. If you feel defensive or protective against some person or group, your amygdala is likely alerting you to a reason to distrust them. If you feel no sense of warning, but instead perhaps cautious curiosity wanting more information, you may be starting from a place of low trust. This is a great opportunity for that person to start demonstrating why you should trust them, to launch the trust momentum in your relationship.

Separate toolsets are required for cultivating trust and easing distrust. You can't improve a distrust situation by using the tools that increase trust. Many people expend great energy toward building or repairing trust by sharing reasons they are trustworthy. However, they are surprised when the feeling of distrust still remains in a protective and aggressive stance. You can't reason with someone's distrust. You must appeal to the amygdala. **Remember, we decide to trust and we feel distrust.**

Our amygdala's job is to save us. Distrust is a superpower that protects us, but it's important to realize it can work to protect us from things we don't actually need protection from (someone from another country), or don't need protection from anymore (childhood trauma with swimming). Although distrust begins as a Guard Dog and dominates trust as it shuts down logical processing and replaces it with primal, instinctive reactions of fight, flight, or freeze,[19] its primary purpose is to keep us safe. When distrust dominates, trust does not necessarily dissipate or disappear. Instead, it is inaccessible until distrust's "all-clear" bark is sounded.

However, if the "all-clear" is rarely sounded, or if distrust is allowed to dominate for too long, the healthy relational tension between trust and distrust is overridden. Paranoia becomes our operating system and many times our Guard Dog becomes an attack dog. Cortisol floods our systems, draining our energy and straining our immune systems. Dichotomy governs our thinking. Civility is withheld, and we villainize anyone who is different. These are the signs of a hyperactive Guard Dog mentality.

The current social climate testifies to this fact. In the past decade, many people have become caught in a downward spiral of hyper Guard Dog Distrust. News cycles that foster binary thinking cause a vortex of bitter, protective anger. However, it's not just the news media; companies, institutions, and brands build entire relationships on lying to us, and it's become far too normal to find out someone is manipulating us. As we gingerly attempt to navigate shifting trust centers, we expend energy in hyper-fight, hyper-flight, or hyper-freeze behaviors. The power of the hyper Guard Dog may be at an all-time high, but trust is not dead. It is just somewhat overshadowed right now. The next question is: **Who let the dogs out?**

Building and restoring relationships while addressing distrust is crucial not only for leaders but also for teachers among their peers. Within the organizational structure of schools, individuals aren't always provided the necessary support to showcase their best selves. Passive aggressiveness can become pervasive, and various conflict management structures may exist within our school systems. However, it's important to recognize that conflict and distrust are fundamentally different. The same approaches used to manage conflict cannot effectively address trust or distrust. We must acknowledge their distinct nature.

While there are policies and procedures in place, such as grievance policies, it's essential to consider situations like a principal's evaluation of teacher effectiveness. How the principal enters that room can profoundly impact the level of trust or distrust experienced by the teacher. If the teacher becomes triggered, it doesn't automatically imply inappropriate behavior. It could simply indicate fear, apprehension about the outcome of their performance evaluation. If the principal lacks awareness of the tools required to manage conflict, mitigate distrust, or foster trust and triggers the teacher, the teacher's response should not be attributed solely to the teacher's shortcomings or issues with students. In reality, the principal has introduced distrust into the environment, and it would be unfair to hold it against the teacher. The teacher's reaction is a natural response, triggered by the release of cortisol in their body.

It all boils down to truly understanding the human dynamics at play. For example, you can trust me as an individual while simultaneously distrusting a particular process. Even if I, as a principal, have established a strong rapport with you, Teacher Smith, and have taken all the necessary steps to cultivate a positive relationship, the inherent distrust of the teacher towards the evaluation process can still lead to triggers. This should not be taken personally. As a principal, it is my responsibility to comprehend this dynamic, be mindful of the signs of distrust, and proactively mitigate its impact. This proactive approach to managing trust is key.

Trust Me:
It's a Dogfight

The Personalities of Distrust

Distrust is almost always viewed as a negative or limiting emotion that should be turned off or ignored. Instead of paying attention to distrust or considering what it might have to tell us, we focus on developing relationships by building trust. Trust is often seen as the hero that has relational superpowers—and it does. However, this doesn't make distrust the villain. The distrust that our amygdala barks is also a superhero when its powers are trained and socialized for healthy reactions.

Distrust has two distinct personalities. Both have one goal: safety. Personality one is the Guard Dog. Personality two is the Guide Dog. *Distrust can act as a guard to protect us in potentially dangerous situations, or as a guide to help us navigate difficult situations.* Recognizing the different personalities of distrust and learning how to use them appropriately is crucial for building and maintaining trust in relationships. The ability to switch between the two can lead to more sustainable and healthy trust. It's essential to recognize that every relationship, whether that's with a friend, spouse, brand, company, or institution starts with risk and distrust, not reward and trust. Every relationship begins with the question, "Do I distrust you?" not "Do I trust you?"

When it comes to dogs, the terms 'Guide Dog' and 'Guard Dog' may seem interchangeable, but the reality couldn't be further from the truth. Guide Dogs are specially trained to assist and protect individuals who are impaired in some way, while Guard Dogs are trained to protect property and deter intruders. But what happens when a Guard Dog, known for its fierce loyalty and protective instincts, is given a new purpose as a guide or companion animal?

A Guard Dog shields us from potential danger. A Guide Dog helps us navigate danger.

When Max, a German Shepherd, was first brought to the Guide Dog training center, the trainers had their doubts. As a former Guard Dog, Max had a reputation for being aggressive and unapproachable. But as the trainers began to work with him, they quickly realized that beneath his rough exterior was a dog with an incredible drive to serve and protect.

Through intensive training and socialization, Max learned to channel his protective instincts positively. He learned to navigate busy city streets, guide his handler through unfamiliar terrain, and even sense and respond to changes in his handler's emotions.

Max's handler, Jane, had been blind since birth and had always relied on a cane for mobility. But with Max by her side, she was able to regain a sense of independence and freedom she had never thought possible. Max not only helped her navigate the physical world, but he also became her constant companion and protector, giving her a sense of security and confidence.

But the transformation didn't stop there. Max's training also allowed him to become a therapy dog, visiting hospitals and schools to bring comfort and joy to those in need. He had come a long way from his days as a Guard Dog, but it was clear that his innate instincts and drive to protect and serve made him the perfect candidate for this new purpose.

As with real dogs, our mental distrust dogs can be trained to act in a manner appropriate to the job we want them to do. Again, they are both designed for a single purpose: safety. However, the path they take to obtain safety is different. A Guard Dog shields us from potential danger. A Guide Dog helps us navigate danger.

PERSONALITY ONE: GUARD DOG

Guard Dogs are trained for one thing: to guard. That seems obvious. However, when someone pushes a Guard Dog too far and is bitten, the surprise somehow becomes newsworthy. The same can be said for Guard Dog Distrust. When we misunderstand someone who's lashing out, because we don't recognize that their amygdala Guard Dog is trying to protect them from something, we may take their behavior personally. This can activate our own Guard Dog protective response, which becomes a downward

cycle of fighting, biting, and protect-at-all-costs—even in a scenario where neither person is actually in any danger.

Ben entered middle school feeling a mix of excitement and anxiety. His older sister had told him her horror stories of what happens in middle school and how "every teacher is out to get you." As Ben walked into his history class, he couldn't shake the feeling that he had to protect himself. He felt isolated and alone.

He sat down at his desk and looked around the room. Everything seemed normal, but he knew from his sister's stories that something was bound to go wrong, and soon. That's when he saw his teacher, Mr. Oden. Ben had heard rumors about him being a tough teacher who didn't tolerate misbehavior.

As soon as Mr. Oden started the class, Ben's amygdala—his Guard Dog—went into overdrive. It perceived Mr. Oden as a threat and began to protect Ben from what it perceived as danger.

"Maybe as soon as a face is there, you know whether to trust it."

Ben acted out in class, not paying attention and even talking back to Mr. Oden. Seemingly he couldn't help it; his amygdala was in control, and it was encouraging him to act in ways that he knew were wrong.

Mr. Oden noticed Ben's behavior and tried to talk to him after class, but Ben was too defensive and mistrusting. He couldn't trust his teacher when his amygdala told him he was in danger.

The Guard Dog runs to protect you so quickly that you're often not aware of what it's protecting you against. It's frequently initiated by microexpressions and microenvironments you're not consciously aware of. You feel danger, but don't know why. And the Guard Dog often protects you so loudly that you can't hear any reasons to calm down or reevaluate, even from your own prefrontal cortex.

Microexpressions: a Guard Dog Whistle

The concept of microexpressions was first introduced by Haggard and Isaacs (1966).[20] Microexpressions are tiny facial reactions a person exhibits as they experience different emotions. These reactions are recognized and interpreted by the amygdala, and the level of distrust is determined within milliseconds. Again, notice we are discussing distrust, not trust. Facial microexpressions are one of the keys to determine how far we will progress in the trust process, and how much we will freely give once we decide to trust.

> *"Janine Willis and Alexander Todorov asked university students to rate the attractiveness, likeability, competence, trustworthiness, and aggressiveness of actors' faces after looking at their photos for just 100ms. The ratings they gave the faces correlated strongly with ratings given by other students who were allowed as long as they wanted to rate the faces. The strongest correlation was for trustworthiness. 'Maybe as soon as a face is there, you know whether to trust it,' the researchers surmised."* [21]

From what we now know about the amygdala, it's more accurate to say, "as soon as a face is there, you know whether to distrust it." When we see a face, the first thing our brain asks is, "Do I distrust this person?" Your face (physical face, company facilities or work environment, brand website, social media platforms, etc.) is your "tell" to the viewer's amygdala. You can't hide these microexpressions from the well-honed Guard Dog. For example, brands, companies, or people whose promises seem "too good to be true" are considered untrustworthy because of their microexpressions. Perhaps their voices are a little too excited, a little too hopeful, a little too happy, and a little too urgent.

It turns out that microexpressions are not only facial but include our entire presence. We emit airborne chemicals that activate alarms in others when we are under stress. Researchers collected sweat samples from individuals experiencing an acute emotional stressor. As a control pool, they also collected samples from people exercising. When the researchers directed people to smell the different anonymous sweats, "scanned participants showed amygdala activation in response to samples obtained from donors undergoing an emotional, but not physical, stressor."[22] When under duress, humans secrete an alarm that wakes the Guard Dog within us, and again we ask, "How much do I distrust this person?" Distrust is something you can literally smell.

Not every situation is dangerous–many are just difficult

Vocal inflection is another microexpression that triggers the amygdala to question distrust. It's not just what we say that can lead a person to be wary of our trustworthiness, it's also how we say it.

"Think about the last person you met who gave you the impression that they weren't trustworthy. Assuming they weren't cackling maniacally, glancing around nervously, or straight-up telling you 'You can't trust me,' there was probably something in their voice that gave it away. According to research, even just a simple 'hello' is enough for you to judge whether you should trust someone or not... Put simply, people trust a 'hello' that has personality. The most trustworthy audio clips offered varied tones: beginning high, dropping in the middle, then rising at the end. The least trustworthy ones were mostly flat, with a slight rise. According to the researchers, if you want people to trust you, put some life in your words."[23]

Distrust's instinctual response to all microexpressions is quick and doesn't take the time to respond with a well-thought-out appraisal. That kind of response is too slow. Calculations take seconds to run, and delay is deadly...at least to a Guard Dog.

AN UNSAFE SENSE OF SAFETY

Our Guard Dog Distrust is crucial for protecting ourselves from unsafe trust options. Our prefrontal cortex, which is responsible for decision-making and problem-solving, tends to be biased toward optimism and may overlook potential red flags in relationships. This often happens because the prefrontal cortex really wants to be in relationship with other people, and it prioritizes making connections. This is where the Guard Dog comes in—it serves as a safeguard, creating an instinctive barrier against potentially dangerous relationships.

However, it's important to note that, like any tool, the Guard Dog Distrust can be misused or become problematic if not properly trained and monitored. An untrained or unchecked Guard Dog can become overly aggressive and turn into an attack dog, where distrust and suspicion are taken to an extreme and impede our ability to form any healthy connections with others. Not every situation is dangerous—many are just difficult, or seem dangerous because of traumatic memories or prejudice, for instance. Training our Guard Dog to know the difference opens a productive path toward the decision to trust.

At the same time, there's also often a clear need for the safety of a Guard Dog. Many circumstances, people, and organizations are obviously out to do harm, or their lack of caring, chaotic leadership, or unrealistic expectations cause harm. Our world is full of hustlers, peddlers, unethical experts and politicians, and marketers seeking to trick you into a simple click. Unilaterally muzzling our Guard Dog limits its resources and effectiveness. The potential costs are high if we ignore the Guard Dog. When risks arise and the Guard Dog barks, shows its teeth, and gets into an attack position, don't scold. Instead, reassure it. Say, "Well done, thank you" and then take note of how much distrust you actually need for that scenario.

Improving our distrust-abilities is a specialized skill that is different from developing aptitudes for trust.

Have you ever been in a job where you come home every night and feel like it's just taking everything out of you? Where the culture is so full of people or environments that trigger your Guard Dog that the toxicity follows you home to infiltrate your relationships, your health, and your time?

Unhealthy distrust costs, especially unhealthy Guard Dog Distrust. Working in an environment that consistently activates your Guard Dog affects your mental and physical health. It lowers work performance and work quality and increases the number of "sick" days taken, and thus sinks the bottom line. When individuals work in a culture of Guard Dog Distrust, they often take it home and create unhealthy cultures of family distrust. Distrust "...robs you of your cognitive resources, hijacks your performance and creativity, and sidelines you from your work (and family).[24] Even if you want to perform at your best, you can't because you're bothered and preoccupied..."[25]

Even though the Guard Dog provides safety, it also walls us off. Distrust can shut us down, often without realizing it. Feedback, interactions, considering problems or errors, and embracing new ideas are all kept at a "safe" distance beyond the wall. We begin to deem everyone and everything a threat. It is essential that we move Guard Dog Distrust to Guide Dog as soon as it's safe to do so.

PERSONALITY 2: GUIDE DOG

Trust needs the friction of distrust to exist, much like stairs need the friction of gravity. Without gravity, you wouldn't need stairs. Distrust provides the friction needed to decide to trust. "The shadow proves the sunshine"—if everything in our lives was known to be reliable and safe, we would have no need to protectively distrust, or make the decision to trust. There is a necessary relational tension between trust and distrust. We don't need to keep thinking of all distrust as unhealthy or bad for relationships! Where a Guard Dog Distrust blocks the path to trust, Guide Dog Distrust maneuvers the path to trust.

It's like the ocean's rip tide or rip current. This is a strong localized current that occurs near beaches with breaking waves. It moves water away from the shore. Although from the surface it appears water is constantly moving toward the beach, under the surface the current is channeling water out to sea. Swimmers and surfers who are caught in a rip current are carried out to sea, no matter how diligently they try to swim toward shore. When used with the proper respect, the current eases the effort and increases the speed at which a surfer can paddle out into the ocean. However, when misunderstood and misused, the rip tide can be deadly.

Similarly, distrust can kill relationships or it can provide a strong current that eases the path to trust. If our distrust controls us, if a Guard Dog is allowed to be the alpha over its master, we cannot experience the power of the distrust-trust partnership. It's easy for us to become controlled by Guard Dog Distrust. However, we are not at our long-term best in a constant Guard Dog state. A dog may seem more powerful when barking and biting, yet we know a dog's strongest position is when providing encouragement, friendship, and guidance. Training the barking Guard Dog to become a stable Guide Dog shifts its power to its superpower.

A Guide Dog is a service dog trained to navigate the environment. The primary responsibility of a Guide Dog is to assist in traversing an unsafe world. This includes stopping when a pause is needed, avoiding obstacles, and finding the way to the decision to trust.

With the help of their Guide Dog, individuals can confidently and safely navigate. The presence of a Guide Dog also serves as a bridge to developing relationships and social interaction. Thus, the Guide Dog is a conduit to the prefrontal cortex and permits a guided decision to trust.

Guide Dogs also play an essential role in increasing independence from amygdala hijack. A Guard Dog amygdala response is loud: high emotion and high energy. The barking is almost impossible to ignore, similar to a triggered trauma response! By contrast, the Guide Dog amygdala reaction is just as instinctive, but it is low emotion and low energy. We still have the choice to ignore the Guide Dog, if our prefrontal cortex decides the scenario is safe enough. We spend more time studying healthy examples of Guide Dog Distrust in Chapter 7.

KEYS TO TAMING DISTRUST: MOVING GUARD DOG TO GUIDE DOG

How can we move our Guard Dog to Guide Dog? One tool is to adapt the same list of "dos-and-don'ts" dog experts use. These ideas are also helpful in relationships, supporting our students, colleagues, and loved ones in recognizing and developing healthy responses.

How to respond to a Guard Dog:	How to respond to Guard Dog Amygdala:
Always reward for appropriate behavior.	Give positive responses and verbalize agreement when you or someone else is right to signal an unsafe scenario.
Always exercise your Guard Dog.	Don't let pent-up energy control the level of response. Physical exercise is the easiest way to reduce cortisol and the overall distrust response when we find ourselves fight-or-flighting from modern "lions."
Always trust your Guard Dog's intuition and instinct.	Learn which gut responses you have are based on facts, and which responses are based on preferences, past traumas, or unproductive biases.
Never pet a barking Guard Dog.	Don't try to force yourself or someone else to "just calm down" when the mind is telling us to watch out! First, clearly listen to and address the thing you are afraid of or angry about.
Never try to distract a barking Guard Dog by feeding it (that only encourages the same behavior).	Complete your fight-or-flight cycle as often as possible through exercise, journaling, meditation, and other techniques, so that your system doesn't get addicted to living in a high cortisol state. Help yourself and others recognize and enjoy the feeling of being calm and safe.

How to respond to a Guard Dog:	How to respond to Guard Dog Amygdala:
Never run away, but don't attack either. Never agitate it to new levels of aggressive behavior.	Often, distrust responses are defensive and aggressive, protectively masking the fear or shame underneath. Learn to look for the foundational reaction, and respond to that, rather than reacting back to aggression with aggression or abandonment: "we'll talk about this when you calm down." The distrust response needs to be heard and understood in order to calm down, otherwise you or the person you're working with just learns to shut down and ignore your own warning signals.

Our goal is not to rid ourselves of the Guard Dog, but, when appropriate, to encourage it to be our Guide Dog as we consider an informed level of trust to share. Guard Dog behaviors are appropriate when the risk level is high. We want our Guard Dog to bark, bite, and attack when necessary. Yet, we don't want the Guard Dog to be the only responder. Our task is to pay attention to our amygdala's responses and consciously decide whether each response is appropriate and healthy or, instead, whether it's based on old trauma or unproductive biases.

Improving our distrust-abilities is a specialized skill that is different from developing aptitudes for trust. The skills needed for distrust revolve around protecting us from risks. The skills needed for trust revolve around choosing to build relationships. Moving distrust from Guard Dog to Guide Dog doesn't necessarily increase trust. We'll discuss increasing trust in the next chapter.

It's essential we understand, develop, and implement strategies that expand our capacity to distrust healthfully and productively. We must know how and when to move Guard Dog Distrust to Guide Dog Distrust. From my research, I've observed that our minds experience a four-stage process while mitigating distrust.

FOUR-STAGE PROCESS WE GO THROUGH WHILE WORKING TO MITIGATE DISTRUST:

1. Experience risk

2. Guard Dog Distrust

3. Move distrust to Guide Dog

4. With distrust as an ally, now the prefrontal cortex can begin deciding on the amount of trust to give

The first stage is risk. Remember "trust, but verify"? Without risk, there is no need for trust. However, we don't go straight from risk to trust. After the instant we experience or perceive potential risk, the first contact our brain makes is with the reactive, Guard Dog Distrust (stage 2). Once the threat assessment is complete, we (hopefully) move Guard Dog Distrust to Guide Dog where it can use its guidance superpowers (stage 3). (Keep in mind, this entire process can happen seemingly instantaneously!) Only after the "all clear" is sounded and distrust becomes a guiding ally is the logical-processing portion of our brains accessible and allowed to decide on the amount of trust to be given (stage four).

Later we will discuss how to build Trust Momentum. For now, the four-stage process for mitigating distrust is only a portion of how we can build trusting relational momentum using the Trust Flywheel (more on that in Chapter 4).

RISK TO TRUST

Our amygdala's job is to persistently intuit risk and assess the appropriate response. It's an enormous front-line responsibility.

I see people's Distrust Dogs assessing risk along a spectrum. The more unfamiliar something, someone, or some experience is, the more likely a person is to react defensively.

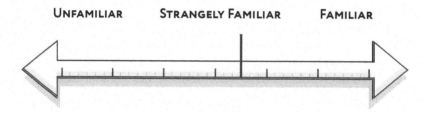

When the risk is unfamiliar, or strangely unfamiliar, the Guard Dog is on high alert. The risk may be too high to allow a move to Guide Dog. During high risk levels, we must be careful trying to muzzle our Guard Dog and moving too quickly to a Guide Dog Distrust. Many circumstances need the loud warning of a good Guard Dog.

There are also many situations when the unfamiliar or strangely unfamiliar pose no risk to us at all. They are simply unfamiliar. However, our amygdala isn't evolved enough to carefully discern the difference—that's not the amygdala's job. For many people, unfamiliar situations induce curiosity and delight, but for others the unfamiliar is threatening. This is often the case when someone's Guard Dog has been on high alert for far too long, with no relief, and they are conditioned to worry if everything new is a threat. We don't need to be surprised when the bark and the bite are the same for high-risk and low-risk unfamiliarity.

If, for instance, you introduce a new concept that doesn't have some form of familiarity, you will receive the not-so-warm welcome of the Guard Dog. Many times, we look back on these kinds of ideas and say the people who introduced them "were ahead of their time." Remember the picture phone? Western

Electric introduced the picture phone at the 1964 World's Fair and rolled it to market in 1970. People hated it. The "picture" in the picture phone was too unfamiliar to be curiously trusted. Or consider the hybrid car. In 1900, Ferdinand Porsche used a battery-powered wheel hub drive and a petrol-gas engine to create the first hybrid car. Again, it was too different for adoption by consumers.

> *Julia Galef, author of "The Scout Mindset," has developed her own analogy similar to our Guard Dog and Guide Dog: Soldier Mindset and Scout Mindset. Soldier Mindset is about enforcing a certain truth or perceived reality, but Scout Mindset is "the motivation to see things as they are, not as you wish they were." She goes on, "Scout Mindset is what allows you to recognize when you are wrong, to seek out your blind spots, to test your assumptions and change course. It's what prompts you to honestly ask yourself questions like, 'Was I at fault in that argument?' or 'Is this risk worth it?' or 'How would I react if someone from the other political party did the same thing?'"[26]*

The Guard Dog doesn't bark as loudly in the presence of familiar and strangely familiar. "In other words, we trust what we know, but we can also trust what we think we know: ideas that are, in fact, quite new but appear strangely familiar."[27] A key to helping move Guard Dog Distrust to Guide Dog is to connect the unfamiliar to the familiar. Providing context eases anxiety and calms the Guard Dog.

Remember the scene in the movie **Hoosiers** where the wide-eyed country basketball team walks into the "big city" arena? Gene Hackman's character assembled the team underneath one of the nets and had them measure the height of the rim and the distance to the foul line. After they completed their measurements, he said, "I think you'll find they are the same as our gym at home." Giving a recognizable connection between the unfamiliar and the familiar motivates the Guard Dog to give way to the Guide Dog.

Whenever Guard Dog Distrust is active, whether it's when you're introducing a new concept or moving to a new neighborhood, it can quickly move to a healthy Guide Dog if given a known reference to imagine. So remember this when you see the hackles of a Guard Dog, whether it's within you or someone else: quickly building links to the familiar will help the trusty Guide Dog to sit beside you.

A MEASURED DISTRUST

The wise counsel of my father to "take a minute" when experiencing fear, anger, or distrust is the best we can do. Giving our mind a "minute" to consider and not just react opens the door to trust. Mostly, we engage in measuring our trust, and an intentionally measured distrust keeps us in control and gives distrust the chance to be the hero by providing guidance.

We measure trust in three dimensions: the level (height), relationship (volume), and environment/context (weight), which we'll discuss fully in the next chapter. We measure distrust the same. When dealing with distrust, it's essential to discern the height to which distrust has risen, the importance of the relationship involved, and the weightiness of each specific circumstance. Assessing the measurements for each dimension provides a clearer picture and helps determine when and how to move Guide Dog Distrust to the forefront.

But how do we assess these measurements in the heat of the moment? The tough news is, it may not be possible in the moment. As we've discussed, the Guard Dog's protective loudness during these situations may suppress all rational thought. However, if in the next moment we can let the prefrontal cortex catch up and process our thoughts and feelings, we may have a chance at a healthy reaction.

Seth Godin supplies a good list of beginning questions to help mindful appraisal:

"Some simple questions worth asking:

1. How does this announcement/offer/news/pressure make you feel?

2. Is there something about this news that touches a hot-button issue or fear? Is the story being told designed to trigger you?

3. Are you surrounded by people who are also engaged with this news? Is it becoming a mob?

4. Is the presenter of the news using external pressure to push you into acting in ways that contradict your self-interest or self-esteem?

5. How would you feel if you discovered that the story you just heard wasn't actually true?

By the time you've asked all five questions, it might be easier to resist what felt irresistible."[28]

These questions can help evaluate:

- Is the height of my distrust at an appropriate level? Too low or too high?

- How does my distrust affect the relationship? Both negatively and positively?

- Given the level and relationship, how much weight does this circumstance deserve?

Measuring is a prefrontal cortex activity and thus develops a path to trust. Knowing how much trust we give defines the relationship we seek to enter. However, measuring trust is complex.

One crucial question we must ask is, "How do we effectively mitigate distrust?" Studies have shown that distrust is primarily alleviated through positive emotional experiences. Mere words like "You can trust me" hold little significance if there is no accompanying emotional connection. In essence, when we emphasize the need to change hearts before changing minds, what we truly mean is that we must address and diminish the existing distrust before individuals are willing to trust enough to learn from one another. While it is possible to acquire knowledge from someone we distrust, deep learning can only occur in an environment where trust is established.

A fascinating concept rooted in neuroscience highlights the physiological and neurobiological impossibility of engaging in profound thinking or deep learning about subjects that do not evoke a sense of personal investment. I can reach a point of caring and concern within a relationship because trust is present in that dynamic. However, when it comes to genuinely caring about a particular topic or subject matter, and engaging in deep contemplation, trust becomes essential. I must trust that the teaching and learning experience I am undergoing will not yield negative consequences. Otherwise, I remain guarded and unable to fully immerse myself intellectually.

Trust Me:
Size Matters

The Complexity of Measuring Distrust

"Whom we trust is not only a reflection of who is trustworthy, but also a reflection of who we are."[29]

We have a bias toward trusting. We want to trust. We need to trust. The prefrontal cortex functions from a deep desire to develop relationships, and the fundamental component of our relationships is trust. As this part of our brain "waits" on the amygdala to give permission, it's like a small child begging for a piece of candy: "Please, please, please...can I trust? Can I trust? Can I trust?... please, please, please."

One key driver behind our trust bias is the evolutionary advantage it provides. Throughout the course of human history, trust has been crucial for survival. Humans have evolved to trust each other and work together in communities. This allows us to develop stronger relationships, find food, and remain safe. And this is true not just of intimate and family relationships; every social interaction is a relationship that we may need for survival, happiness, or success. As a result, we have a natural trust bias that predisposes us to believe the best about others...and ourselves.

Another factor that contributes to trust bias is social influence. People tend to trust those around them and follow their lead. This is especially true when it comes to people we admire, respect, or feel a sense of affiliation with. You are more likely to check out a new restaurant in town after hearing a glowing review from a friend who's eaten there already.

The psychological benefits of trusting others can also fuel trust bias. Trusting others helps to reduce stress and anxiety and can promote a sense of safety and security. People who trust others are often more optimistic and have a more positive outlook on life. Additionally, trust can lead to greater feelings of connectedness and community, which can boost our overall well-being and happiness.

However, our bias can encourage us to rush into trusting too much or too quickly. It can push us to ignore the warning of distrust. Our trusting belief in others can be misplaced. We can be fooled into respecting the wrong person, and our drive to be happy and have relationships can cloud our judgment about when and how much to trust.

Furthermore, it's crucial to understand that personal experiences, culture, and media can influence our trust bias to withhold trust. If we've had negative experiences with people who share a certain characteristic (e.g., race, religion, gender, etc.), our bias may lead us not to trust other people who fit that description, even if they have not personally done anything negative and our amygdala hasn't warned us against trusting them. Our prefrontal cortex can archive predetermined lists of reasons to trust and to withhold trust. These lists exist to shorten the time it may take to decide and to manage the calories our brain uses to process, but they can also mislead us.

The decision to trust is complex. But trust isn't an all-or-nothing proposition. It's a matter of degree and extent. Trust usually isn't a binary "yes" or "no" question. It's a question of how much and to what extent. The decision to trust is nuanced by the manner in which we measure it.

THE SCALE AND THE STICK

The figure below displays the common notion that trust and distrust are interrelated and have a direct impact on each other, like items weighed on a scale. As the figure illustrates, many people think a decrease in one results in a corresponding increase in the other. So, as trust decreases, distrust increases.

Similarly, we may see trust and distrust on a spectrum, as opposite ends of a single continuum. If we've never had a reason to think about how trust and distrust work, there's an automatic assumption that the more trust we feel, the less distrust we must feel, and vice versa.

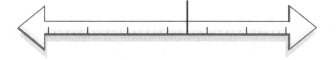

This binary construct promotes trust as "good" and distrust as "bad." It also presupposes that the definition of a good relationship is one that banishes every ounce of distrust to gain 100% trust. Often, distrust is seen as a disorder that needs psychological correction, an archenemy to be defeated at all costs. However, as we learned in the last chapter, distrust plays a vital role in underpinning healthy trust. Every interaction and transaction and every relationship requires both trust and distrust.

What happens when levels of trust and distrust are detached from each other and allowed to move independently? Trust and distrust often do have an effect on each other, the brain processes them independently. When we understand trust and distrust are autonomous, we can begin to use both at the same time as resources for building, repairing, and sustaining healthy relationships. Without both, we lack the tools to manage disappointment, recover from victimization, and forgive betrayal.

	LOW DISTRUST	HIGH DISTRUST
HIGH TRUST Characterized by: ▫ Hope ▫ Faith ▫ Confidence ▫ Assurance ▫ Initiative	- High-value congruence - Interdependence promoted - Opportunities pursued - New initiatives	- Trust but verify - Relationships highly segmented and bounded - Opportunities pursued and down-side risk/vulnerabilities continually monitored
LOW TRUST Characterized by: ▫ No hope ▫ No faith ▫ No confidence ▫ Passivity ▫ Hesitation	- Casual acquaintances - Limited interdependence - Bounded, arms-length transactions - Professional courtesy	- Undesirable eventualities expected and feared - Harmful motives assumed - Interdependence managed - Preemption: best offense is a good defense - Paranoia
	LOW DISTRUST Characterized by: ▫ No fear ▫ Absence of skepticism ▫ Absence of cynicism ▫ Low monitoring ▫ No vigilance	**HIGH DISTRUST** Characterized by: ▫ Fear ▫ Skepticism ▫ Cynicism ▫ Wariness and watchfulness ▫ Vigilance

Lewicki, McAllister, and Bies charted the character of high and low trust and distrust. The table above can be used as a tool to both understand and chart the trust and distrust mixture at any point in a relationship.

> "Trust and distrust both entail certain expectations, but whereas trust expectations anticipate beneficial conduct from others, distrust expectations anticipate injurious conduct."[30]

Discovering that trust and distrust are autonomous provides a wealth of insight, which we'll explore through the rest of the book. For starters, we're going to evaluate trust as if it is a three-dimensional object.

How much do you trust someone?

From my research and observations, we can measure trust along three different metrics. The amount you trust is measurable by concepts similar to height, volume, and weight.

Height measures how tall an object is, usually in linear units. Volume measures how much space an object takes up, often in cubic units. Weight is a measure of the force exerted on an object due to gravity, usually measured in units such as kilograms or pounds. We experience trust similarly.

Height can be used as a measurement of trust in terms of how much confidence one has in a particular person or situation. Height is easily obtained and given. It is also unstable and easily toppled if it is the only factor in your trust experience. We often give a great depth of trust to someone or something very quickly, and then take it away very quickly. However, if merged with volume and weight, the height at which trust is experienced is almost immovable.

Volume can be used as a measurement of trust in terms of the amount of information or experience one has with a person or situation. How much space does this trust relationship take up? How many trust experiences have I had with this person or situation? And for how much time? Volume is very stable. Yet, if it's a mile wide and an inch deep or isn't very weighty, it may take up a lot of space but not be very meaningful.

Weight can be used as a measurement of trust in terms of the impact or importance of a particular person or situation in one's life. For example, a person may have a high level of trust in a family member or close friend, as the impact or importance of these individuals in their life is significant. On the other hand, a person may have a lower weight of trust in a stranger, as the impact or importance of this person in their life is much less. The greater the impact or importance, the greater the weight of trust.

MEASURING TRUST - APPLICATION

It might be helpful to think of trust as water in a three-dimensional container. The water can be measured by the level (height) it reaches, but it can also be measured by volume (gallons). When considering the third measure, weight, we must consider gravity. Gravity determines the weight of water so in a context with less gravity, the water will have a different weight.

How does this relate to measuring trust? Let's say you get into an Uber with a driver who has a trust "height" of 6. Perhaps you would say you trust your friend from third grade with the same trust height. Are you experiencing the same quality or amount of trust for your Uber driver as for your childhood friend? Not likely. The level or height that trust reaches is only one measurement. The volume of trust for the Uber driver is just minutes, where the volume of trust for your friend spans decades. In addition, the richer and more robust the relationship, the heavier the "context" of the relationship, and the more trust "weighs." Thus, the trust for your friend you have spent a lot of time with is more stable and secure than the trust for the Uber driver you are only seeing once.

However, there are some contexts where the Uber driver's container of trust might weigh more, even though it's "smaller." For example, perhaps your friend is a terrible driver, or is blind and can't drive, or has a history of drinking and driving. The weight of trust is measured in weightiness via context. In this example, you would trust an Uber driver with great reviews to drive you more than you would trust your good friend behind the wheel.

So, how much do we trust? It depends on the level (height), relationship over time (volume), and context (weight). Several factors determine the level (height) that trust reaches. Yet, for our purposes, we can simply consider that level (height) is achieved by a perceived correspondence between recorded experiences and the situation at hand. It's what Rachel Botsman calls "strangely familiar." When there is a strange familiarity, we recall past experiences to quickly judge the level (height) to which trust rises.

We require familiarity to begin to trust. Without it, distrust builds a wall of protection. When someone tries to get you to eat an unknown meat, they will comfort you by saying, "It tastes like chicken." Why? Because chicken is a familiar, almost-tasteless meat that is at least tolerated by most people. Chicken has a pleasant recorded experience around which the mind can develop trust for the new. It's a "safe" taste trust baseline.

So, if something is "strangely familiar," how quickly can you trust? Can you trust someone in just a few seconds? Minutes? Hours? Of course, the answer is, "It depends." We have the ability to trust to a certain degree within seconds, and the level (height/depth) may rise quickly. This is good news for someone launching a new product, someone relying on episodic encounters (think Uber or Airbnb again), a blind date, or for teachers and students on the first day of a new school year. However, this trust can be unstable. Its "container" lacks the wide experiences (volume) that may be needed to stabilize the trust.

When we say, "Trust takes time," it's this volume measurement we're talking about. Volume is achieved through more exclusive encounters with the object we trust. Increased relational capital deposited in our mind creates trust relationships with greater volume, and these relationships become more stable and tougher to influence. The more relationship over time (volume) exists, the greater the consequence when the level (height) drastically changes. For example, when a couple divorces because an affair is suddenly discovered, or when journalists reveal that long-

established banks fraudulently loan money for their own gain. No matter how much volume, a lot or a little, the structure can fall given the right scandal.

Sometimes (more often than we like to admit), we trust strangers over relationships (volume). How is this possible? Weight. As we discussed previously in the example of our Uber driver and our friend, weight, or context, is the gooiest of the three measurements. We have difficulty rationalizing how it works, but we require its influence daily.

Context gives trust weightiness. In many cases, context (weight) trumps both level (height) and relationship (volume). We trust a proven, bot-driven algorithm when deciding on a stock purchase before we trust the home-spun advice of our mother. We'll let a waiter take our credit card behind closed doors and yet hide it when our kids come for a visit. We trust Google Maps to get us to our destination over the "wisdom" of a veteran New York taxi driver. Context is king when it comes to trust.

CONTEXT IS EVERYTHING: THE PROXEMICS OF TRUST

Many of us would enjoy weighing ourselves on the surface of the moon. We would weigh significantly less. However, if you compared your weight on the moon to your weight on Earth, influenced by Earth's gravitational pull, it would bring up completely different feelings.

When words or actions are taken out of context, they can be misinterpreted and create a different story. For example, a sarcastic comment made to a friend may be misconstrued as hurtful if taken out of context, or if spoken to a stranger. Context is everything when it comes to understanding and interpreting things.

The context in which trust is given is the gravity determining how much weight it carries. To better understand trust, it's helpful to have a framework that can give insight into the different contexts and gravitational options available.

Proxemics: the branch of knowledge that deals with the amount of space that people feel is necessary to set between themselves and others.

In the '60s, Edward Hall developed a communication theory based on proxemics. He proposed that we communicate in four spaces (contexts): Public, Social, Personal, and Intimate. In 2003, I published a book, *The Search To Belong*, building on Hall's work with a simple twist. I asked, "If we use those four spaces as a framework for communication, can we also assume we search to belong within that framework?" It turns out, Hall's communication theory provides an excellent structure for understanding how we seek to belong.

It also turns out that Hall's framework provides insights into the contextual references we use to measure/weigh trust. Remember, trust seeks relationship. Relationships and belonging can be organized within Hall's four contextual spaces. Therefore, the four spaces give us insight into the context of trust.

We trust differently within each spatial context. Many times we trust without much thought, especially in contexts that require fleeting (low volume/time) relationships. Walking across a crosswalk, having dinner in a restaurant, jumping in a cab, making small talk during a social event, and performing most of our everyday activities require us to quickly trust at a high level because of the context/weight of the scenario, but don't require us to trust for long periods of time/volume. It may be helpful to see these as fleeting spikes of trust.

There are contexts, however, that require a lot of trust and trustworthiness (height/depth) over a reliable, long relationship (volume/time). Friends, partners, business teams, and students all hope that we are trustworthy, and trust us with volume and weight.

Have you ever entered a small elevator where a person is continuing the conversation they were having with their colleague before you entered? Didn't they receive the memo? When riding in an elevator, all conversation must stop until you exit or you are in the elevator alone with your colleague. An elevator is a public space, and to continue a social, personal, or (God forbid), intimate conversation is "wrong" or at least very uncomfortable for most.

> *"Social scientists of the most varying standpoints agree that human action can be rendered meaningful only by relating it to the contexts in which it takes place. The meaning and consequences of a behavior pattern will vary with the contexts in which it occurs. This is commonly recognized in the saying that there is a "time and a place for everything."*[31]

It seems simple. However, humans are complex, and how we develop trust and trustworthiness is like walking on shifting sand as the ocean currents ebb and flows. As Edward Hall discovered in his communication proxemics, space (context) is constructed in the mind. Of course, the outside environments influence how we build contextual spaces in our minds, but it doesn't always match the interpretation of those around us.

We also have the ability to switch back and forth between these contexts without missing a step. Often that step is without notification, warning, or a hint asking the other party to move with us. Sometimes we mentally trade spaces without knowing it ourselves. So, when trust is developed or expected within a specific context, we can't depend on it to stay there, and we often can't determine where it's moved. We've all experienced scenarios where a lighthearted visit shifts suddenly to something much more serious, from a social trust environment to an intimate trust environment.

The following four spatial contexts for trust can be used to recognize and cultivate healthy senses of community and relationship at the various appropriate levels. The gravity of the kind of trust exchanged changes with each shift between contexts.

Public Trust

Public trust is given because of an outside resource or experience. I give a high level of trust to an oncoming driver because there's an outside resource guiding us to behave in specific patterns: the law. When taken out of my usual context, the story changes.

My first experience of traffic in India called into question all the patterns I'd learned and I questioned my ability to trust anyone, including myself, on the road. Drivers in India do not trust each other based on a set of governmental rules, laws, or protocols. They drive with the trust of bees swarming in a hive. Dividing lanes, stop signs, turn lanes, and speed signs are only references and are usually ignored.

Or when I'm at the airport, and I run into another fan of my favorite team, Indiana University Hoosiers, we might be delighted to exchange notes on the upcoming season. This generally won't lead to exchanging names and numbers and carrying on a relationship. We just happened to exchange trust with each other in a very casual, impersonal way for a brief period of time.

High levels of public trust are essential to living within a society. We depend on others to generally follow social norms, and we, in turn, develop trustworthy behaviors and actions that also fit with a social contract.

However, a public trust context doesn't provide or require much weight. It's necessary, and we must have the skills to maneuver within the public context, but when the relationship has a weightier impact on our life, public trust context isn't the answer. Public trust is about connecting with a mutually-shared outside resource, and social trust is a discovery process by which I want to connect with you.

Social Trust

Social interactions play a key role in forming, strengthening, and preserving relationships. The context of social situations provides the necessary foundation for establishing "snap-shot" trust, which creates a quick bond or allows for a quick disconnect without damage. When networking at social events, trust is built based on the importance of the gathering and the potential of the relationship. Finding the right balance of trust is crucial in establishing a new relationship, and the social context is a fertile ground for exploration at a safe distance. We can begin to find the sweet spot: not too little trust as to be unstable, but not so much trust as to be inappropriately intimate too soon.

Developing the skills for giving social trust unlocks the prospects of finding new friends, family, and partners. Because of these possibilities, social contexts carry a more significant weightiness than public contexts.

Personal Trust

The ability to safely share private information is the hallmark of personal contexts. At this point, it's necessary to establish the difference between private information and intimate information. The difference can most readily be observed from the point of view after the information has been shared. When inappropriately shared, private information hurts the party it's concerning, but it's not devastating. Intimate information, on the other hand, destroys the person it concerns. The difference is the weight felt by each context.

The weight of personal contexts creates stability and drives longevity. Relationships have resilience and strength. They power through difficulties and thrive on protecting each other. Because the context provides weight, personal context relationships are not easily eliminated.

Intimate Trust

An intimate context is the weightiest of all four because it requires two unique ingredients. First, it requires a safe place to share "naked" experiences or information. Naked doesn't refer to nudity only. It refers to the open and unveiled quality of the experience shared. The second ingredient is "unashamed". When naked information or experiences are shared, and there's no shame involved, intimate weight is accomplished.

As we seek relationships in each of these contexts, we experience a distinctive weight furnished by each. And this weight influences how we feel and measure trust.

The convergence of trust height, volume, and weight, along with the four trust contexts, form solid groundwork for evaluating and cultivating trust. Nevertheless, there is another crucial element that necessitates consideration: trust momentum. Trust momentum encompasses the trajectory and velocity at which trust is either developing or diminishing over time. In the upcoming chapter, we delve into the power of the Trust Flywheel.

Trust and distrust can coexist simultaneously, as they originate from different regions of the brain. It's possible to distrust certain scenarios, actions, or individuals within an environment while simultaneously trusting in the potential for a different outcome in the future. This complexity means that in order to feel secure, it's not necessary to eliminate all elements of distrust. Rather, the focus should be on creating or experiencing a prevailing sense of trust. In the school setting, I can trust that my teacher possesses expertise in the subject matter and that they will invest extra time and effort to support my learning. However, I may still have a lingering distrust that a mistake I make will have irrevocable consequences, as everything feels high stakes.

Measuring the completeness and complexity of trust reveals that trust is influenced by the duration of the trust relationship and the significance of the matter being entrusted. Research in American education highlights the compounding positive effects of teachers who follow students across multiple years. This continuity fosters a relationship that deepens over time, akin to that of a lifelong friend. Additionally, the level of importance attached to the matter being entrusted plays a crucial role. For instance, although we may not have known our heart surgeon our whole life, we trust them with our lives, forging a profound level of trust.

In the realm of education, we often underestimate the impact of our actions or inactions on students. What may seem trivial to adults holds outsized importance for children. Take, for example, a middle-school student experiencing their first heartbreak. An adult's response might dismissively encourage them to move on. However, an empathetic teacher who acknowledges the child's pain, offers sympathy, and reminds them of their inherent worth generates an abundance of trust. This intense and significant experience for the child garners numerous trust points, creating a lasting impact.

However, it's essential to recognize that the perception of importance lies in the eye of the beholder. To respond in a way that nurtures trust, it requires genuine humility and time. Trust-building is a gradual process that holds true across various contexts. Establishing trust with individuals or entities that have little reason to trust, such as students let down by the education system, demands even more time and effort.

Trust Me:
It's All About Momentum

Discovering The Trust Flywheel

Momentum is a force to be reckoned with. In the physical world, momentum can be defined as "mass in motion." All objects have mass; so if an object is moving, then it has momentum—it has its mass in motion. The amount of momentum that an object has is dependent upon two variables: how much stuff is moving and how fast the stuff is moving."[32]

Momentum is also an invisible fuel that propels a team or athlete to victory. Attributes like talent, skill, knowledge, athleticism, and effort have little consequence compared to momentum. Momentum energizes performance and aids in overcoming insurmountable obstacles. When a team or athlete has it, they can quickly bounce back from mistakes and setbacks. A team that can maintain momentum is better able to perform well under pressure. The power of momentum can be the difference between a win and a loss, and it's why so many coaches and athletes develop strategies to gain and maintain it throughout the game.

When athletes have momentum, they become more confident in their abilities and are able to push through adversity. This increased confidence can lead to better performance, as they are more likely to take risks and make bold moves. In fact, studies have shown that an athlete with momentum is more likely to win.

When listening to a game's broadcast, the commentators almost always mention that a team must get off to a good start, begin the second half with a bang, or end the game well to have a chance at winning. During the final minutes of a game, a coach or commentator often mentions the need for a momentum-swinging play. Good teams plan and strategize momentum swings. Average teams hope for them.

The same is true for developing trust. Trust development requires momentum. Good leaders, teams, organizations, personal relationships, and classrooms have plans and strategies to obtain and maintain trust momentum. Average leaders blindly hope for trust momentum. Good leaders plan and strategize for it.

> *A flywheel is a mechanical device that stores rotational energy by spinning around a central axis. It is typically made of heavy materials like steel or cast iron and can be found in various applications, from industrial machinery to the engines of vehicles with manual transmission.*
>
> *The energy stored in a flywheel can be used to smooth out fluctuations in power output or maintain a steady rotational speed. In some cases, it can also be used to provide backup power in case of a power outage or other disruption.*
>
> *Flywheels are also used as an analogy in various contexts to visualize the concept of momentum or inertia. The idea of a "flywheel effect" suggests that once something starts gaining momentum, it becomes easier to maintain that momentum over time. In the context of relationships, the Trust Flywheel provides a framework for developing and maintaining trust momentum in a relationship and how to diagnose when there's a breakdown.*

Mr. Hubbard, a 10th-grade math teacher, is well aware of the power of momentum. He has a challenging 2nd-period class filled with students who have struggled with math in the past. Mr. Hubbard knows that if he could build trust momentum with this class, they would be more likely to overcome their obstacles and achieve success.

He began the year by focusing on developing trust before pushing too much new content. He took the time to get to know each of his students and was open and approachable. He made sure to listen to their concerns and to provide positive feedback when they accomplished something. His class quickly trusted him and each other.

Good teams plan and strategize momentum swings. Average teams hope for them.

Mr. Hubbard also built momentum during each class period by beginning each class with an activity that lowered distrust. He furthermore made sure to stop mid-way through the class to check in on students' trust levels and planned "bounce-back" trust activities to quickly recover from setbacks when students might be triggered by challenging concepts or memories of past failures. At the end of the day, Hubbard ensured that each student knew he trusted them to accomplish the tasks he'd given them so the class could maintain their momentum into the next day.

The key to developing trust is to access the power of momentum. Understanding and employing the Trust Flywheel provides access to that energy. However, we first must understand the stages of a relationship to see how the Trust Flywheel functions within those steps.

Relationships gain momentum by moving through four distinct sequential stages, and each stage is critical for the relationship's progression. Exploring the four stages of relationship building and how they relate to the three phases of the Trust Flywheel provides a framework for developing and maintaining trust in a relationship, and by understanding its three phases, we can build momentum and better navigate the stages of relationship building.

IT'S ALL CHUTES AND LADDERS

Every relationship moves through four stages. These stages are sequential, none can be skipped, and—much like the children's board game, Chutes and Ladders—our progress can be interrupted, and we can abruptly find ourselves beginning again at stage one.

THE FOUR RELATIONAL STAGES ARE:

1. Distrust
2. Curiosity
3. Engagement
4. Commitment

DISTRUST

For a long time, marketers have crafted ads to guide us through the four stages quickly. Marketing agencies know we are predisposed to distrust the products and companies they promote. Therefore, they attempt to mitigate our distrust before building trust or getting us to commit. They skillfully send messages through images, music, or words to encourage us to feel safe. Marketers also specifically discover and intentionally respond to the aspects of their product or company that people may instinctively distrust.

Anyone attempting to develop trust in any relationship must also begin with discovering, addressing, calming, and mitigating distrust. Relationships never begin with building trust.

Mr. Hubbard, who so successfully builds momentum in his math classroom, didn't always understand these dynamics. Early in his teaching career, Mr. Hubbard started his first day at a new school excited to meet the students and ready to kick off the new year. He met his first day with anxious excitement. Based on his own experience with math and the aspects of math that motivated and attracted him, he was prepared to jump head-first into a challenging problem he was sure would keep his students' attention for days. He had the perfect plan.

Mr. Hubbard trusted that his degree had prepared him. He trusted that, for the most part, students attended school to learn. He trusted that students in this particular school had engaged, supportive parents. Basically, Mr. Hubbard trusted that his first day would be every teacher's ideal.

For reasons Hubbard wouldn't discover until later, most of his students showed up to math class with a high degree of distrust. They didn't trust the school. They didn't trust they could learn the material or pass the tests. And worst of all, they didn't trust their math teacher could get them through it. Mr. Hubbard's lesson plan was built on the idea that his students would be curious and would quickly engage and commit themselves to the study of math. But curiosity can only flourish in an environment where we feel safe enough to explore. Because of their previous math class failures, Hubbard's students showed up already distrusting that environment and their own capacities to learn.

Maybe we should teach future educators the way we train future marketers. The first question the brain processes is, "How much do I distrust?" All relationships begin with this intuitive evaluation from the amygdala. It is crucial to understand that everyone with whom you develop a relationship naturally begins their evaluation of you with distrust. It is necessary and healthy for them to get their amygdala's approval before continuing the process of relationship building and trust development.

You must get them to distrust you differently.

When someone initially distrusts you, it isn't primarily about you. You may be completely trustworthy and have a beautiful resume or impeccable reputation, but your credentials will help later on, with building trust. Distrust is an intuitive safety measure designed to protect us against harmful relationships.

Your first goal isn't to get someone to trust you, but to aid them in mitigating their natural distrust of you. You aim to relax their amygdala and move the barking Guard Dog Distrust to a watchful Guide Dog Distrust. Notice your goal isn't necessarily to get them to distrust you less. You must get them to distrust you differently. If you try to skip this stage, you may be in for future barking and biting sessions.

Curiosity

Once the process of discovering and calming distrust has begun, the environment feels safe enough to move to the next step in relationship-building: curiosity. Curiosity is a powerful tool for building trust in relationships. When genuinely curious about someone, we are more likely to see them as complex, multi-dimensional, and interesting, rather than as frustrating, mysterious, or alarming. This encourages us to engage our prefrontal cortex's executive thought. This perspective shift can help in the decision to trust.

However, it is essential to note that not all curiosity is created equal. Manipulative or insincere curiosity can reinforce feelings of distrust, as it may be perceived as an unsafe tactic to gain information or control. Genuine curiosity, on the other hand, is an open and honest desire to learn and understand. This type of curiosity activates both the amygdala and the prefrontal cortex, which are involved in emotional regulation and decision-making. Together, these brain regions help us navigate the complexities of relationships and develop trust.

Today Mr. Hubbard begins each year, and each class session, with activities that stir students' curiosity. "I was sitting on my couch watching a football game, and as my favorite team was once again losing by a touchdown, the announcer said, 'They need a momentum-swinging play.' I said out loud, 'That's what I need for my classroom!' and I wondered what I could do that would swing the momentum of my failing lesson plans. The next thing I stumbled upon was an exercise that piqued their curiosity, and I knew I'd found the answer. I now spend 75% of my prep time finding activities that stir curiosity, and when they work and my students become curious, I know I'm 75% of the way to getting them to engage in learning."

When curiosity is activated, we naturally seek to engage. The more we learn about the object of our curiosity, the more we feel connected to that person, concept, product, or company. This feeling of "knowing" nurtures a desire to solidify the connection.

Engagement

As we traverse the bridge between curiosity and engagement, we experience the prefrontal cortex beginning its work. The executive brain creates logical reasons to continue or disengage. Logical thought always begins with the questioning inquiry of curiosity. After all, there's no need for the brain to spend calories building a list of reasons to trust if curiosity isn't present. You may have decided you don't need to distrust a person or experience, but that doesn't mean you want to have anything further to do with them. Only after you become curious do you begin to desire engagement.

Engagement is a stage of discovery, questioning, wonderment, and experimentation. Engagement is the building of logical lists, equations, and answers to the questions posed by curiosity. It is also the stage where belonging is formed. Engagement requires a relational answer to "Can I trust and belong?" and "If so, where/how?" Engagement matures within a prosocial community, not in a void.

Over years of focusing his lesson plans on curiosity, Mr. Hubbard noticed that "once a student becomes curious, they automatically seek someone to share it with. I rarely need to plan a way to put students into groups. They place themselves in 'Curiosity Teams,' and that drives a high level of engagement."

During the Engagement stage, we see the first exhibition of relational trust. Our brain has concluded that the next step is worth the risk. Whether that step is to ask a question, habituate brand loyalty, give someone a helping hand, purchase a product online, or jump into an Uber car with a stranger, we are cautiously entering a relationship.

Engagement is usually a magical time; however, it is also the most fertile ground for failure and disappointment. During this stage, we can experience a time of discontent, disappointment, and even hopelessness. We may begin to wonder if the journey is worth the effort or if the problem is solvable. We might consider the opposition too big, or that we've been fooled into believing it can be defeated. The Guard Dog Distrust begins to rear its head again. How we respond to this valley of potential failure determines if we progress to commitment or return to stage one, distrust, and begin the process again.

Engagement starts, and ends, with relationship and community.

During the engagement stage of a new school year, a student may feel excited about the possibilities and potential opportunities that lie ahead. However, as the weeks progress, the workload may begin to feel overwhelming, and the student may start to doubt their ability to succeed. They may wonder if the effort required to succeed is worth it.

At this point, the teacher can play a crucial role as a support system for the student. By encouraging curiosity and empowering the student to lean into their challenges without fearing failure, the teacher can help the student maintain trust momentum and progress to the next stage of commitment.

The teacher can help the student to identify and mitigate potential sources of distrust, such as negative self-talk or limiting beliefs. They can also focus on building trust momentum through destigmatizing ambiguity, creating an environment where their student feels free of shame, and has agency to try things and fail.

Commitment

The final stage is marked by a decision to move forward and not go back. Commitment puts a stake in the ground and says, despite the potential of future distrust, curiosity, and engagements that follow, we will move forward. Commitment is a decision to continue continuing. This final stage isn't final because the other stages never emerge again, it's final because it's no longer as fragile as the others. Commitment learns how to calm the Guard Dog during the Distrust stage, generate its own curiosity, and remain engaged even when the plot sags. This isn't to say this stage is impenetrable, but it usually takes a proportionately catastrophic event to change its status.

During his 20+ years of teaching, Mr. Hubbard has seen it all, tried it all, succeeded, and failed at it all. And the one thing that his students know is he's committed to them and their learning. He's still walking through the stages with his students each year, period by period, and he has chosen to commit.

Moving from one stage to the next isn't just about how our brain processes; it's also about developing an artful momentum that carries us through. How do we create the momentum to move safely through the relational stages?

Trust.

Trust is the element that carries relational energy and, even in the worst of circumstances, can develop lasting and productive relationships. Trust is the glue that bonds us together through the stages.

> "Relationships defined by trust, openness, and exploration of ideas move teachers, students, and schools forward...and will ultimately build the future of this country."-Kevin Baird

Understanding the building blocks of trust development stems directly from the relational stages. Each stage is a cornerstone in the Trust Flywheel and shows why trust is the essential element to building relationships. As we build momentum through the Flywheel, our relationships deepen and become stable.

THE TRUST FLYWHEEL

The push-pull relationship between trust and distrust can generate volatility. Generally, that's the last thing we want to increase in our everyday lives. Instead, we prefer a steady diet of stability and consistency, and our decision to trust is rooted firmly in the hope of predictable and unshakable experiences. Yet, paradoxically, volatility and risk provide an energy that fuels trust.

LEARNING REQUIRES RISK, WHICH MAKES LEARNING FERTILE GROUND FOR TRUST.

Whether you're an administrator, teacher, or student, situations requiring trust development have the same three-part structure. The first stage is mitigating distrust. Notice we didn't say erasing or eliminating distrust. Distrust is always present in healthy trust development. As we said above, our goal is to get people to distrust us differently—more healthfully and productively.

STAGE ONE: MITIGATE DISTRUST

Like we saw in Chapter 2, distrust has two "personalities" that help keep us safe. The first is the personality of a Guard Dog. The second is that of a Guide Dog. For trust to develop, distrust must move from Guard Dog to Guide Dog. As the amygdala moves toward being a guide for the decision to trust, distrust is mitigated, and the prefrontal cortex is released to do its work of executive thought and decision-making. This movement energizes the process to trust.

Personality Traits of Our Dogs

Guard Dog

- Physical, mental, social, and emotional protector

- Stands on guard, ready to bark and exhibit aggressive behaviors

- Well-trained, a Guard Dog is not an attack dog but loudly warns us

Guide Dog

- Decision-guide and protector

- Agreeably watches for new threats

- Well-trained, a Guide Dog nudges us to safety

Mrs. Hernandez was a dedicated middle school principal who spent her entire career working to improve the lives of her students. She was always eager to take on new challenges and initiatives, but she never expected the challenge presented to her by the superintendent, Dr. Rose.

One day, as Mrs. Hernandez sat in her office, Dr. Rose knocked on the door and asked if she had a moment to talk. Curious about what her boss wanted, Mrs. Hernandez invited her in.

Dr. Rose began by explaining that there was a growing population of immigrant families in their district who did not speak English as their first language. She had a plan to start an ESL program for these families, but she needed the help of someone who was respected in the Hispanic community, passionate about education, and had a proven track record of success.

Mrs. Hernandez was intrigued by the idea, but she had concerns. Her first reaction was to say "No." She was worried about how she would find the time and resources to start; even more, she was frightened and unsure about how she would be able to connect with the families, some who were living on the streets.

Dr. Rose understood these concerns and asked about her own experiences with ESL programs and her thoughts on how they could be adapted to meet the needs of immigrant families. She also asked Mrs. Hernandez what resources she would need to make the program successful and how they could work together to find those resources.

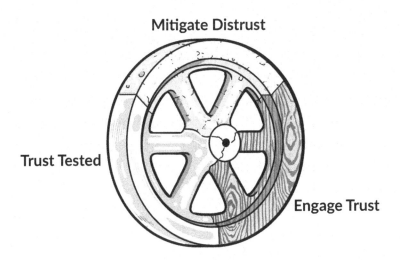

These efforts demonstrate the importance of moving from Guard Dog to Guide Dog to mitigate distrust and energize the process of trust. By engaging her Guide Dog, Dr. Rose could employ Mrs. Hernandez's trust and work with her to develop a plan that would benefit the community. The next step in their relationship is for Mrs. Hernandez to begin choosing to trust Dr. Rose.

STAGE TWO: ENGAGE TRUST

As soon as we move our relationship from distrust to curiosity, we engage trust, the second Flywheel stage. As we've mentioned, trust is a decision formed in the prefrontal cortex. Trust engagement begins when this part of our brain begins considering the reasons we should and shouldn't extend trust. As we've noted previously, this is largely automatic and even unconscious. Our Guide Dog sits under our feet, watching as we carefully list each item for consideration. The trust process is engaged, and momentum begins to build.

As Mrs. Hernandez and Superintendent Rose talked about ESL classes, Mrs. Hernandez began to see the program's potential and built trust in Dr. Rose's vision. She began to think more deeply about the reasons why and why not to extend trust, and Dr. Rose helped her consider the pros and cons of creating an ESL class for the local immigrant community. As they considered each item, Mrs. Hernandez began to see how this program could be a powerful tool for helping the community and began to feel a sense of momentum building.

Mrs. Hernandez agreed to take on the initiative and worked closely with Dr. Rose to make the program a reality. Thanks to their collaboration and trust, the ESL program became a huge success, and both Mrs. Hernandez and Dr. Rose were proud of the impact it had on the community.

Notice how the Trust Flywheel engaged as Mrs. Hernandez's Guard Dog Distrust started out with reasons not to participate in the ESL program. Dr. Rose displayed her own curiosity by asking about Mrs. Hernandez's experiences. Her curiosity encouraged Mrs. Hernandez to become inquisitive. They moved the Flywheel forward by using curiosity as a bridge from mitigating distrust to engaging trust.

STAGE THREE: TRUST TESTED

Once we decide to trust, the next step, Test Trust, will eventually emerge. Often this step takes us by surprise. We've considered the pros and cons and weighed the risks, and our Distrust Guide Dog intuitively agreed with our decision. And yet, trust must be tested for it to mature and deepen. It's essential that we maneuver through this stage of trust development. Without it there is no momentum, no developing risk, that increases the energy that's needed for sustained trust.

As trust is tested, the Guard Dog Distrust shows up, often barking and biting, and the process begins again. We must mitigate new distrust and find a way to engage trust again. This is how the Trust Flywheel builds momentum.

As Mrs. Hernandez and Dr. Rose worked closely, they bonded and found a collaborative flow. However, it wasn't without challenges. Just as the project began to require more time and energy, an emergency happened in the district that divided the superintendent's attention. At first, Mrs. Hernandez didn't think much about spending unplanned time to cover for Dr. Rose. But the stress wore on her, and she needed help. There were several late nights when she became frustrated with Dr. Rose's absence. She often felt taken advantage of and all alone.

At the same time, her prefrontal cortex reasoned with her that Dr. Rose would of course be much happier working on their ESL passion project than the problems of the day that were drawing her away. Mrs. Hernandez was confident that the superintendent's late night texts encouraging her and apologizing were sincere.

Fueled by her frustration of not being there at critical moments, Dr. Rose wondered if Mrs. Hernandez was making the correct decisions. She questioned Mrs. Hernandez's motives as people in the community began reporting back about the project. Along with Mrs. Hernandez, Dr. Rose had to choose to continually mitigate her distrust and re-engage trust. In the end, the two became closer and more trusting because they worked through the minefield of testing trust. The Trust Flywheel gained speed and momentum.

THE FLYWHEEL EFFECT

Flywheels are amazing sources of energy. A flywheel builds and stores kinetic energy, and with each revolution, more energy is generated. Flywheels are designed to rotate at high speeds. They are typically connected to a power source that provides the initial energy to start the flywheel spinning. As the flywheel gains momentum, the energy stored in the flywheel keeps it spinning and can be used to power other devices, such as generators or motors.

Our desire to connect with people, concepts, services, companies, and products supplies the Trust Flywheel with the initial energy needed to start spinning. As it gains momentum, the Trust Flywheel provides the power to move through each relationship stage. As in the case of Dr. Rose and Mrs. Hernandez's relationship, its energy also smooths the jerkiness of the starting and stopping caused by the volatile relationship between trust and distrust.

The Trust Flywheel's initial revolutions may be subconscious as the amygdala rapidly vets through microexpressions and environments. The subsequent rotations become more conscious as we become more aware of the amygdala's work. Thus, the stakes go up with each cycle until the Trust Flywheel is smoothly providing energy—or until its momentum is abruptly interrupted and trust is broken.

Within the first few interactions, we move from the subconscious and low risk to more conscious and higher risk. After the Guide Dog appears and we decide to trust, we may test that trust more consciously. The "Test Trust" stage moves us above the subconscious line into consciousness. Now the risks are higher. As the revolutions continue, the Trust Flywheel gains momentum, and both risk and consciousness seep back below the subconscious line.

As we move through the relational stages, the Trust Flywheel rotates with increasing speed. During stage one, Distrust, the Trust Flywheel is moving slowly and deliberately. It emerges from the subconscious and is highly visible during the Curiosity stage. It ebbs and flows during Engagement and, as the Trust

Flywheel effect returns to the subconscious, it marks the move from Engagement to Commitment.

There are many words we use to describe how trust is obtained. Earned, built, developed, acquired, cultivated, nurtured, strengthened, won, constructed, forged, grown, formed, secured, achieved, established, committed...you get the point. In whatever form you use to express the existence of trust, there are three primary concepts you must consider:

Trust is a Process

Trust doesn't have an ending point. It's never finished, or full up. Trust is a dynamic process that takes energy to maintain and sustain. Trust isn't a construction project with schedules and an end goal. Trust is relational instead of mechanical, fragile instead of permanent.

Trust is Both Controlled and Uncontrollable

As the prefrontal cortex uses its superpower to reason and decide, there are elements that are in our control. However, that's just one stage within the Trust Flywheel. We can quickly lose control as the Guard Dog emerges to keep us safe. The instinctive quality of the amygdala and the speed at which it reacts is out of our control. And during the testing stage, we often don't initiate or control the test. Trust is a relationship between what we can control and what we can't, and that process is a gift of ambiguity, wonderment, and frustration.

Trust is Developed Collaboratively

Trust is collaborative. We develop trust with each other. The trust process is more a dance than it is an accountant's spreadsheet or a contractor's building. This explains why many "trust" programs often don't develop sustainable trust. Most use a building or earning model instead of a developmental model. Trust develops in the everyday. It is not primarily built or earned during a workshop or program. Just because I fall into the arms of my coworkers during a trust fall doesn't mean I'm going to trust that they'll come through on a promised deadline. Trust doesn't obligatorily deepen over time. It develops within the Trust Flywheel process.

Then What?

Trust is a dynamic process that requires effort and energy to maintain and sustain. It involves both controlled and uncontrollable elements, as we navigate the dance between our reasoning prefrontal cortex and instinctive amygdala. The Trust Flywheel provides a helpful framework for understanding how trust develops and evolves through the different relational stages. As we move through these stages, from distrust to engagement and ultimately to commitment, the Trust Flywheel gains momentum and rotates with increasing speed.

Trust is developed collaboratively through everyday interactions and experiences rather than through one-off programs or workshops. By understanding the trust process and the role of the Trust Flywheel, we can work to cultivate and strengthen trust in our relationships with others. What can be done when trust momentum breaks down? Similar to developing trust, recovering from broken trust is a process: both trust and distrust are involved.

Testing trust involves displaying unwavering consistency. A remarkable real-life example can be found in Clark County, the fifth largest school district in the nation.

The administrators' union passed a vote of "no confidence" against Superintendent Dr. Jesus Jara. In most cases, superintendents would seek opportunities elsewhere when faced with such a situation. However, Superintendent Dr. Jesus Jara took a different path. He stood firm in the face of the vote, insisting that his number one priority was student success. The underlying conflict stemmed from significant tensions with the principals' union, as Dr. Jara had placed substantial pressure on principals who held great autonomy. Ironically, Dr. Jara was one of the most ardent advocates for principals that one could encounter. Advocacy, however, does not preclude holding individuals to high standards. Dr. Jara's unwavering stance led the school board to launch a culture study led by the board chair, an action which, in the end, resonated with the community.

Dr. Jara's unwavering stance led to an actual investigation, which resonated with the community. All conversations about the desired changes were ultimately centered on the well-being of the students rather than the system itself. Dr. Jara often used the phrase, "I don't give a damn about the system. I give a damn about the students." He firmly believed that the system should serve the students, but frequently, it became focused on catering to the adults. As a result, the Clark County district not only rescinded the initial vote of no confidence but extended Dr. Jara's contract and even granted him a raise. Testing trust means standing up and proclaiming, "No, I represent the community, their interests, and if you fail to recognize that, we will shed light on the matter."

Trust is regularly put to the test by students who inadvertently present opportunities for trust to be lost. Teachers, in turn, have multiple choices in how they respond. Sometimes, students test boundaries as they navigate their new environment, attempting to gauge the extent to which they can push and observing your

> *reactions. Other times, trust is tested when students find themselves in moments of vulnerability, seeking support and assistance. Conflict, often forgotten, is one of the primary ways in which trust is tested. In a recent John Wick movie, a powerful quote resonates: "Friendship means little when it's convenient." Similarly, trust, akin to friendship, reveals its strength during times of need. It is crucial to understand that trust is challenging to test without encountering conflicts—it is within the crucibles of life that trust is truly examined.*

Trust Me:
I Let You Down

Dealing with Broken Trust

*"I am not upset that you lied to me,
I'm upset that from now on I can't believe in you."*
—Nietzsche

Mrs. Eager has always been a beloved teacher to her 6th-grade students. She is known for her enthusiasm and dedication to her class, and her students look up to her with admiration and respect. However, things took a turn for the worse when Mrs. Eager unknowingly started showing favoritism toward a particular group of students. Some students were given preferential treatment and extra attention, while the rest of the class felt ignored and unimportant. Some students were allowed to turn in work after the deadline had expired. Mrs. Eager also rearranged class seating, and the same students moved to the front of the classroom.

Jenny, one student who felt ignored, noticed this unfair treatment and started to lose trust in her teacher. Jenny is an above-average student who enjoys the social environment of Mrs. Eager's class. Sadly, over time, she began questioning Mrs. Eager's motives and stopped participating in class altogether. She felt that Mrs. Eager was not treating everyone fairly and that her hard work and engagement were not being acknowledged. The atmosphere in the classroom became tense, and Jenny was no longer excited to come to class and learn.

The situation came to a head when Jenny approached Mrs. Eager and asked her why she didn't like her any longer. Mrs. Eager tried to brush it off, but Jenny insisted on an explanation. Mrs. Eager could not provide a satisfactory answer, and her relationship with a considerable portion of her class was damaged. Jenny could no longer trust her, and the classroom that had once been a place of learning and fun became a place of tension and distrust for any students outside the favored group.

YOU LET ME DOWN

Everyone has experienced the letdown and turmoil of broken trust. The emotional disruption of betrayal can leave us feeling hurt, guarded, and defensive. We develop feelings of suspicion and distrust toward others, making it challenging to open ourselves up to new relationships, or rebuild existing ones. The damage to our sense of trust, in ourselves and our own judgment, can also lead to feelings of insecurity and self-doubt.

"Broken trust" may have very little to do with trust. Instead, it often stems from the disappointment we experience when someone or something fails to meet our expectations. This disappointment triggers a response in our amygdala, shifting our mindset from being guided by trust to becoming guarded and defensive. Our Guard Dog re-emerges and our brain's executive function may be impaired, leading to a shutdown of rational thinking. We become disenchanted because the trust momentum we built comes to a halt, and the future we envisioned is shattered.

The element of the relationship that breaks during broken trust is trust momentum, not necessarily trust itself. The level of trust may remain the same. However, as distrust's voice becomes louder, and trust momentum is slowed, the trust we may feel melts into the background. In order to move into repair, we need to be giving attention and energy to the feelings of distrust.

Because this experience is felt so deeply, we often think trust cannot be easily regained, and it can take a lot of time and effort to rebuild it. However, understanding the mechanisms of distrust can aid in the speed of the healing process. By recognizing how our distrust arises, how it affects our actions and reactions, and how it can be trained or untrained, we can work toward repairing broken trust momentum in a more efficient and effective manner.

The possibility of broken trust is a natural part of the Trust Flywheel as it progresses through the three stages of the trust-development process. The first step toward effective trust repair habits is accepting that broken trust is natural, and we can recover. While trust is an essential component of any relationship, it is constantly being challenged in large and small ways, and can be broken at any point in the journey, particularly during the Trust

Tested stage. Trust is not a fixed state, but rather a dynamic and ever-evolving process that requires constant effort to maintain and repair.

The good news is, testing trust doesn't necessarily lead to broken trust. For Mrs. Eager and Jenny, trust was tested as Jenny felt abandoned and suddenly out of place. Notice that there is a point where testing trust turns into broken trust. Jenny summoned the courage to confront Mrs. Eager about her changing behavior. At this point, Mrs. Eager had the opportunity to keep the Trust Flywheel moving by acknowledging Jenny's concerns, and then helping her mitigate distrust. Sadly, that's not what happened this time. Probably out of embarrassment, Mrs. Eager brushed Jenny off. It's this failure during the testing stage that often leads to broken trust momentum.

While broken trust can occur for various reasons, like the aftermath of a lie, a betrayal, or a simple miscommunication, the process needed to repair and recover broken trust is the same. Thankfully, Mrs. Eager can still repair the relationship with Jenny, and the class, and get the Trust Flywheel moving again. But let's not get ahead of ourselves. Let's first examine what we are experiencing as broken trust.

WHAT IS BROKEN TRUST?

Similar to developing trust, recovering from broken trust is a process. Both trust and distrust are involved. Initially, we've worked to mitigate distrust, and our executive brain has built lists of reasons why we should decide to trust. Then trust is tested, and perhaps broken. Broken trust is when the Trust Flywheel is abruptly interrupted and comes to a screeching halt. Because we've moved through the first two-thirds of the Flywheel and we are confident in the method our brain uses to develop trust, broken trust always catches us by surprise. More times than not, we are unprepared.

For most, when we feel caught off guard, we feel foolish—we "should have known better." And when we feel foolish, we become defensive. Confidence quickly fades to confusion. The trust momentum generated isn't just slowed, but destroyed. Broken trust is experienced when the prefrontal cortex is shown to be a fool for deciding to trust, and the amygdala's Guard Dog comes to the rescue by developing a heightened climate of caution.

Jenny's courage to confront Mrs. Eager melted into feeling foolish, unseen, and unimportant. Where she once felt energized and special, she now "knew" she had misinterpreted her place in the class and with Mrs. Eager. Although Mrs. Eager's self-protecting response may have been a miscommunication, Jenny's real experience was broken trust and a broken relationship.

The speed at which trust is tested and broken can make it even more difficult to cope. It can happen without warning and leave us feeling blindsided and unprepared. It can also seem like the smallest, most innocent action or expression curiously tests or breaks trust. As you can see, trust is both strong and fragile.

Both parties in this story experienced unfortunate breakdowns in their distrust/trust mechanisms. Mrs. Eager's inconsiderate and defensive response to being called out was a protective reaction from her Guard Dog Distrust. Her amygdala was barking, "Warning! Don't be vulnerable with your student! You should distrust that Jenny will keep respecting you if you admit your mistake!"

As we develop the awareness that trust, in all our relationships, goes through testing periods, over and over again as a natural part of the Trust Flywheel, we empower ourselves and others to react in a healthy, productive way. It's another tool in our tool belt for training our reactive Guard Dog into a helpful Guide Dog. A willingness to take responsibility for one's actions, to listen actively, and to communicate vulnerably and honestly can help in the repair process. Individuals and organizations can restore the foundation upon which their relationships are built and move forward in a positive direction by taking the necessary steps to understand and repair broken trust. Understanding the underlying factors that break trust is also a key to sustainable repair.

WHY DO WE SO QUICKLY BREAK TRUST?

It is human to distrust. Our amygdala is so quick and in tune with the possible danger that surrounds us; it's human nature to be quick to feel broken trust. Trust is built on a relationship with the unknown and, thus, on a foundation of vulnerability, making it difficult to maintain. When we trust someone, we are putting ourselves in a position of vulnerability and opening ourselves up to the possibility of being hurt. This exposure significantly contributes to the Guard Dog's protective response. Trust can instantly be broken if we feel violated. When the unknown is revealed differently than we had expected, or our vulnerability is taken advantage of, our barking Guard Dog Distrust emerges, and trust is compromised.

Jenny's initial experience of Mrs. Eager making their classroom prosocial, engaging, and inclusive allowed her to open up and be vulnerable. She trusted Mrs. Eager to act consistently. She believed that given every chance, Mrs. Eager would embrace her and everyone in the class equally. Notice that Jenny didn't instantly break the trust bonds they had developed. She gave Mrs. Eager a chance to recover from the mistake of showing favoritism by confronting her teacher and asking her what was going on.

Broken trust is when the Trust Flywheel is abruptly interrupted and comes to a screeching halt.

Historically, Jenny's experience with Mrs. Eager wasn't one of betrayal, which could have made her more cautious and standoffish. Jenny experienced Mrs. Eager's class as a safe place. However, Jenny could have past experiences with others that contribute to a hyper-awareness of being left out and excluded. These could provide Jenny's Guard Dog with memories of needing protection. Jenny may have built up defense mechanisms to protect herself from being hurt again, making it difficult to maintain trust with others.

Trust is complex and fragile, and it makes me wonder why we bother with trust at all. Our desire to trust and be trusted is at the core of every relationship. So why do we so quickly act in a way that jeopardizes trust?

Why? Because we're human.

We quickly act in a way that jeopardizes trust because we're human. The natural interaction between the amygdala and the prefrontal cortex is foundational to our motivation to both protect ourselves and develop relationships. These two assignments can be at odds. When situations arise that put our safety at risk, the Guard Dog barks, and when our strong need and desire to develop a relationship exists, we desire to trust. When they arise simultaneously, which they often do, we behave oddly.

> I present the thesis that human beings are naturally predisposed to trust—it's in our genes and our childhood learning—and by and large it's a survival mechanism that has served our species well. That said, our willingness to trust often gets us into trouble. Moreover, we sometimes have difficulty distinguishing trustworthy people from untrustworthy ones. At a species level, that doesn't matter very much so long as more people are trustworthy than not. At the individual level, though, it can be a real problem. To survive as individuals, we'll have to learn to trust wisely and well. That kind of trust—I call it tempered trust—doesn't come easily, but if you diligently ask yourself the right questions, you can develop it.[33]

Mr. Humphrey taught high school English for more than 20 years, and he built a reputation as an excellent teacher who was dedicated to helping his students succeed. However, when the school principal, Mrs. Roberts, introduced a new policy that required teachers to grade assignments on a strict deadline, Mr. Humphrey's amygdala perceived it as a potential threat to his ability to provide quality education to his students. He felt this policy would force him to rush through grading assignments, which could lead to inaccurate evaluations of his students' performance.

Mr. Humphrey began to avoid communicating with Mrs. Roberts, instinctively trying to protect his autonomy and take the time he needed to grade well. Because the principal didn't know why Mr. Humphrey was distancing himself, this behavior created tension and distrust in their relationship. Mr. Humphrey began to criticize and distrust everything Mrs. Roberts did. Both of them began to expect the worst from one another. Truth Telling became subjective, and they went out of their way to share their exaggerated points of view with others.

What if Mr. Humphrey had instead taken the time to evaluate the situation with his prefrontal cortex? He might have realized that Mrs. Roberts' new policy was intended to promote fairness in the grading process. If he had turned toward the principal in the test trusting moment, rather than turning protectively away, he could have provided valuable feedback on improving the policy to benefit all the students and teachers.

These situations seem cut and dried from the outside. Why wouldn't Mr. Humphrey decide to process primarily with his prefrontal cortex? It's hardly ever this easy. More times than not, the amygdala is trying to protect, even while the desire to keep the relationship is strong. Perhaps in this case, Mr. Humphrey had past experiences where the principal didn't heed his concerns about a new policy, which set him up for a swift return to distrust behaviors. The interaction between the amygdala and the prefrontal cortex is often at odds. This interaction can lead to quick and seemingly illogical actions that put trust in jeopardy.

But What If It Was Your Fault?

There are many origins of broken trust. Most involve our expectations and the letdown when they are not met or attacked. Let's discuss one of the most common, lying, as an example of how our Guard Dog Distrust. Lying crushes trust momentum more quickly than almost any of the other letdowns. Understanding the motives helps us mitigate distrust more effectively and use specific remedies to repair broken trust.

WE LIE BECAUSE WE ARE HUMAN

We lie to convince people to trust us. That sounds odd, because we know that deception actually erodes the trust we develop with others. Mainly we lie for two reasons. In many situations, telling the truth may not produce the most favorable outcome for us. Telling the truth might lead to negative consequences, such as losing a job or damaging a relationship. By lying, we can present ourselves in a better light and increase the likelihood of others trusting us. We lie to keep the relationship while protecting ourselves.

The second reason we lie is to gain power and control over others. By manipulating the truth, we can manipulate the actions and decisions of those around us. We manipulate them into trusting us. This can be particularly effective in situations where we need to exert influence over others, such as in the workplace or in politics. For example, a salesperson may lie about the features of a product in order to make a sale, even if it means potentially breaking the trust that has been established with the customer. Similarly, in a job interview, a candidate may exaggerate her qualifications in order to land the job, even though it could lead to distrust in the long run.

Whether it's to keep ourselves in a better light or to gain an advantage, we lie to build trust, and, unsurprisingly, men and women lie differently.[34] Men and women each test trust by attempting to influence a different region of other people's brains. It seems that generally, men lie to make themselves look good, and women lie to make others feel good about themselves.

In broad sweeping strokes, men appeal to the prefrontal cortex to encourage others to decide to trust them. They focus on giving reasons, true or not, for others to decide to trust them. Women, on the other hand, stereotypically, appeal to the amygdala when lying and hope others distrust them less. Women primarily focus on lies that will lower the bark of the Guard Dog's distrust. They may ignore lists of reasons to trust and instead concentrate on actions that lower distrust. This is a significant difference. In general, men think to feel, and women feel to think. The "lying-to-build-trust" strategy of each targets the brain region with which they are most familiar.[35]

> *Though adult men and women lie in roughly equal numbers, they diverge in the types of lies they tell: Men tend to lie in an attempt to appear more powerful, interesting, or successful than they are. They tend to lie about themselves eight times more than they do about others. Women lie more often to protect other people's feelings or to make others feel better about themselves. Numerous research papers contend that women become more uncomfortable when telling lies than do men. When telling serious lies, women described themselves as more guilty, anxious, and fearful than the men did. There is some evidence that over time, as women get to know each other, they read their female friends' deceptive ways more accurately than their male counterparts do with their male friends. Those least likely to lie have strong same-sex relationships and score high on psychological tests regarding responsibility.*[36]

The way that men and women approach building trust differs. Women tend to focus on reducing distrust through emotional appeals and personal anecdotes. Conversely, men tend to provide logical reasons and evidence to convince others to trust them. This distinction is important to remember when working to establish or repair trust in relationships, as different strategies may be needed for each gender.

Understanding these differences can help us navigate the complex dynamics of trust and deception in our relationships and interactions with others. It also aids in our efforts to repair broken trust.

PERSONALITIES DRIVE HOW WE TRUST AND DISTRUST

Whenever topics that deal with human behavior are discussed, like trust and distrust, inevitably, someone will ask, "Does personality and/or gender affect your conclusions?" What they are really asking is, "I'm too complex to fit in your neatly tied-up box...how do you account for me?" And, to a degree, they are correct. All human behavior is contextual and complex.

> "The purpose of the Myers-Briggs Type Indicator® (MBTI®) personality inventory is to make the theory of psychological types described by C. G. Jung understandable and useful in people's lives. The essence of the theory is that much seemingly random variation in the behavior is actually quite orderly and consistent, being due to basic differences in the ways individuals prefer to use their perception and judgment.
>
> "Perception involves all the ways of becoming aware of things, people, happenings, or ideas. Judgment involves all the ways of coming to conclusions about what has been perceived. If people differ systematically in what they perceive and in how they reach conclusions, then it is only reasonable for them to differ correspondingly in their interests, reactions, values, motivations, and skills." (Jung)
>
> In developing the Myers-Briggs Type Indicator [instrument], the aim of Isabel Briggs Myers, and her mother, Katharine Briggs, was to make the insights of type theory accessible to individuals and groups. They addressed the two related goals in the developments and application of the MBTI instrument:

> 1. The identification of basic preferences of each of the four dichotomies specified or implicit in Jung's theory.
>
> 2. The identification and description of the 16 distinctive personality types that result from the interactions among the preferences."[37]

> "The Enneagram is a system of personality typing that describes patterns in how people interpret the world and manage their emotions. The Enneagram describes nine personality types and maps each of these types on a nine-pointed diagram which helps to illustrate how the types relate to one another.
>
> According to the Enneagram, each of the nine personality types is defined by a particular core belief about how the world works. This core belief drives your deepest motivations and fears—and fundamentally shapes a person's worldview and the perspective through which they see the world and the people around them.
>
> Our core beliefs are not necessarily incorrect, but they can be limiting and operate as 'blinders' for people. Understanding our Enneagram type and how it colors our perceptions can help us to broaden our perspective and approach situations more effectively.
>
> Understanding a person's Enneagram type helps us to see why they behave the way they do. Each Enneagram type has a set of core beliefs that will consistently motivate them to take particular actions and guide them to make certain decisions. Behavior that may seem confusing or contradictory can often be explained when we understand a person's Enneagram type.
>
> The Enneagram also helps us understand how people react to stress. By describing how each Enneatype adapts and responds to both stressful and supportive situations, the Enneagram shows opportunities for personal development and provides a foundation for the understanding of others."[38]

So, where are the cracks in the "box" that allows individuality to push through and contextualize how people trust and distrust? Primarily it has to do with speed. Personalities and genders influence the speed at which we decide to trust and feel distrust, the speed of recovery and repair once trust is broken, and how we practice and process sustainable trust in our relationships.

For example, men are slower to trust and slower to repair broken trust than women. Some personalities feel their own distrust as heartbreaking, while others feel their distrust is protecting them. Learning to be aware of these differences gives us superpowers for navigating relationships, mitigating distrust, and building trust.

We all naturally desire to protect the way we see ourselves and the way we see the world. Personality-type theories, like the Enneagram and Myers-Briggs, can provide insight into the motivations behind why different individuals may choose to break trust or increase distrust in a relationship.

For example, according to Enneagram theory, individuals with a type 8 personality, also known as Challengers, may be more likely to break trust intentionally, as a desire for control and power. They may be willing to manipulate or deceive others in order to achieve their goals, and to maintain dominance in a relationship.

Similarly, according to Myers-Briggs theory, individuals with the ISTJ personality type may be more likely to break trust as they tend to be more closed-off and reserved, which can make it difficult for them to build and maintain trust in relationships.

On the other hand, those with a type 9, known as the Peacemaker according to Enneagram theory, may be more likely to betray trust unintentionally as they try to avoid conflict and may prioritize decisions that please others.

It's important to note that these theories are not definitive, individuals may have a mix of personality traits, and it's hard to generalize the behavior of one individual based on the personality type. It's also important to note that regardless of the personality type, many different motivations can lead to the breaking of trust in a relationship. (For additional insight see table on pages 146-148)

Dr. Martinez, the school superintendent, is an Enneagram 9, known as the Peacemaker. She has a strong desire to maintain harmony and avoid conflict, which can lead to her making decisions that please others rather than standing firm on her convictions. This can unintentionally betray the trust of those she works with, such as Mr. Boggs, a parent on the school board who is an Enneagram 8, known as the Challenger. Mr. Boggs is driven to control and have power in situations, and may use these desires to achieve his goals.

Mr. Boggs often seems like a bully to Dr. Martinez as he fights for his convictions. Dr. Martinez's Guard Dog amygdala is often aroused to distrust. She feels taken advantage of as he demonstrates bulldozer tactics to push his agenda during meetings. Dr. Martinez thinks she appears wishy-washy in these situations, and believes Mr. Boggs looks powerful. Dr. Martinez wants others to see her as fair, calm, and collaborative. Mr. Boggs wants to seem smart, strong, and as having leadership potential.

Dr. Martinez and Mr. Boggs have different motivations for breaking trust and increasing distrust in their relationship. Dr. Martinez may make decisions that please Mr. Boggs even if it goes against her beliefs, while Mr. Boggs may try to manipulate and deceive Dr. Martinez to achieve his goals.

Mr. Boggs wonders how you can trust someone who is so wishy-washy, and Dr. Martinez can't believe anyone would go along with someone like Mr. Boggs, who can't collaborate and only wants to get his own way. The truth is they both want things their own way.

Our personalities stem from our view of the world and how we want it to operate. When we use our personalities, we protect the world as we see it. Our Guard Dog barks when the world doesn't cooperate with how we believe it should function. When we encounter another personality (view of the world), our amygdala is on high alert, and distrust is elevated.

It's important for Dr. Martinez and Mr. Boggs to understand their motivations and how they may affect their relationship. Both need to be aware of their own personality traits and how those may influence their behavior to mitigate distrust and develop sustainable trust in their relationship.

Repairing trust reside in the three stages of the Trust Flywheel. The momentum of the Trust Flywheel reacts directly to the effectiveness and consistency with which we engage the three stages of the flywheel. Our effectiveness and consistency are often swayed by our personality, our circumstances, how we were socialized as children, and a host of other factors. It's essential to be self-aware and vulnerable while moving our Guard Dog to Guide Dog, collecting the necessary information to decide to trust, and as our trust is tested.

NOW WHAT?

Human nature plays a significant role in how we perceive and act in situations that jeopardize trust. Our amygdala and prefrontal cortex constantly interact, which can lead to quick and seemingly unexplainable actions that erode trust. However, understanding the dynamics between the two can help us navigate these situations more effectively and provide a path to develop a momentum of trust.

Using this information, we can employ the Trust Flywheel framework as a structure for understanding how to repair trust in any given situation.

In the next section, we will delve deeper into the Trust Flywheel and explore practical strategies for repairing trust in various situations. By understanding the Trust Flywheel and its elements, we can learn to navigate the complexities of trust and build strong, lasting relationships.

WE REPAIR BECAUSE WE DESIRE RELATIONSHIP

Chang Ming, a high school senior class president, is known for his leadership skills, positive attitude, and academic excellence. However, mid-semester, he had a conflict with Mr. Hamilton, his social studies teacher. The rift began when Mr. Hamilton assigned a group project in his class and Chang was placed in a group with students who he felt were not taking the project seriously. Despite his efforts to motivate and encourage his group members, the project was not completed to his satisfaction. He then went to Mr. Hamilton to express his frustration and disappointment with the group members. He also questioned Mr. Hamilton's decision to group them together. Mr. Hamilton felt that Chang was too hard on his classmates.

This led to a few heated exchanges between the two in class, with Mr. Hamilton feeling that Chang was being disrespectful and Chang feeling that Mr. Hamilton didn't understand or care about his experience. As a result, Chang felt like Mr. Hamilton began to grade him more harshly, and his grades in that class began to drop.

Chang's classmates and other teachers noticed the tension between him and Mr. Hamilton and questioned the situation. Mr. Hamilton, who wanted to maintain the relationship with his model student, decided to take steps to repair the broken trust and address the issues with Chang.

Repairing broken trust is a complex process requiring careful attention to both trust and distrust. It is not enough to focus on one or the other. As Mr. Hamilton pursues repairing trust, he can't stop at lowering the heightened distrust Chang Ming has, nor can he only focus on raising the level of trust. Mr. Hamilton must use specific tools for each of the Trust Flywheel's three stages, over and over again.

FOUR STEPS TO REPAIR

Repairing broken trust works best with a dedicated effort from all parties involved. However, by following a few key steps, it only takes one of the parties involved to influence the possibility of repairing broken trust and rebuilding a strong, healthy relationship.

STEPS TO REPAIRING BROKEN TRUST:

1. *Assess* your current state: Realize the depth of your own distrust and the role it may be playing in the relationship. Acknowledge and mitigate your own distrust and lean on the desire to continue the relationship.

2. *Act* in a way that mitigates the distrust of the other: Work to move their Guard Dog to a Guide Dog.

3. *Access* relational tools that lead the other to a decision to trust

4. Be *Aware* that trust will be tested again and again: Be prepared for these tests, and continue to work on rebuilding trust.

STEP ONE: ASSESS

The first step in repairing broken trust is to assess your current state. This means first realizing the depth of your own distrust and the role it may be playing in the relationship. This step is crucial for rebuilding trust as it allows you to take responsibility for your actions and understand their impact on the relationship. If Mr. Hamilton tries to help Chang Ming mitigate his distrust before taking care of his own Guard Dog Distrust, he will not only be unsuccessful but may create a dependent-codependent relationship. It's the same as when the flight attendant instructs you to put on your oxygen mask before helping others. Only by acknowledging and mitigating your own distrust can you begin to lean on the desire to continue the relationship.

For instance, if Mr. Hamilton feels insecure about Chang's reliability, it's important to acknowledge that this insecurity may be causing his Guard Dog to bark loudly and impede trust. Mr. Hamilton may relentlessly question, check up on him, or grade too harshly. By acknowledging these feelings and working to mitigate them, Mr. Hamilton can begin to rebuild trust by showing Chang that he is committed to the relationship and willing to change.

Secondly, Mr. Hamilton must remind himself of how important the relationship is with Chang. The decision to trust stems from a desire to have a relationship. When trust is broken, it can be easy to want to give up on the relationship. However, if you value the relationship, it is crucial to put in the effort to repair the trust. This means being open to difficult conversations, being willing to apologize and forgive, and committing to the process of rebuilding trust.

STEP TWO: ACT

The next step in repairing broken trust is to act in a way that mitigates the distrust of the other person. This means working to move their Guard Dog to a Guide Dog. Remember, this doesn't necessarily mean you are lowering distrust. Instead, you are working on getting them to distrust you differently. One of the best ways to do this is by being transparent and open with your actions. This means being honest about your intentions, feelings, and thoughts. When the other person feels like they know you are not hiding anything, they are more likely to let their guard down.

Another way to mitigate the distrust of the other person is by being consistent in your actions. Consistency puts the Guard Dog to sleep and allows the Guide Dog to emerge. This means keeping your promises, being on time, and being dependable.

If Mr. Hamilton shares with Chang Ming how the groups were chosen and how he might change the selection in the future, he will likely be successful at relaxing Chang's Guard Dog. If Mr. Hamilton can also show how he can be consistent in his grading practices, it's possible that Chang's Guard Dog will stop barking. Only by acting in ways that mitigate Chang's distrust can Mr. Hamilton begin to move to rebuild trust.

STEP THREE: ACCESS

The tools to develop trust include techniques that access the prefrontal cortex by encouraging decision-making, reasoning, social seeking, and other executive thought processes that lead to relationship. It's key to understand these are not the same as the required tools to mitigate distrust. Trust develops in the presence of curiosity, and when agency is promoted, ambiguity looms, and fast failure is celebrated. As Mr. Hamilton encourages Chang Ming to move his barking Guard Dog to a focused Guide Dog, he can begin to access the tools that drive Chang's decision to trust.

> In the education context, "fast failure" refers to a strategy of encouraging students to take risks and make mistakes as a way to learn and improve. This approach emphasizes that failure is a natural and necessary part of the learning process and that students should not be afraid to try new things and take risks. By embracing failure as a learning opportunity, students can develop a growth mindset and become more resilient and adaptable learners. Teachers who adopt a "fast failure" approach may provide frequent feedback and encourage students to reflect on their mistakes and use them as a way to improve their understanding and skills.

Mr. Hamilton can encourage Chang Ming to openly ask, "Why?" The ability to safely question the motives and reasons behind decisions allows the prefrontal cortex to seek relational depth. Vulnerability drives understanding, which not only keeps the Guard Dog at bay but delivers critical support for relationship.

Mr. Hamilton could also invite Chang and the class to have input in selecting the groups that will work together. Giving agency allows the executive brain to sift through equitable group selection, promoting decision-making and relationship development.

Using specific tools that promote relationship and decision-making creates an environment for trust. Most models try to build trust by focusing on deflating distrust. These tools will only get you a quieter Guard Dog. They don't move to the next step of building and developing trust. It's critical to gain momentum by both mitigating distrust and engaging trust.

STEP FOUR: AWARE

It's essential to remember that rebuilding trust is not a one-time event but a continuous process. Once we decide to trust again, a testing phase will inevitably re-emerge. This cycle is necessary for momentum to develop in the Trust Flywheel. As Mr. Hamilton and Chang Ming decide to trust again, they will experience their trust being tested. The more keenly they are aware that this is a necessary stage of trust development, the more they will fluidly move the Trust Flywheel ahead and with additional velocity.

THE BRAVEST THING YOU'LL EVER DO IS TRUST AGAIN.

This process can take time. However, it's not necessarily true that it takes time to trust again. We decide to trust, and thus, we can decide at any moment. What usually takes time is mitigating the distrust we feel. As we practice this process, the Trust Flywheel gains momentum, and the rebuilding time is shorter.

The bravest thing you'll ever do is trust again. When you lose trust momentum, it takes fortitude, grit, and vulnerability to get it moving again. However, the good news is that it's possible. Recognize how to use specific tools during each stage while navigating with the Trust Flywheel. Soon you will be back on track, building momentum in trusting yourself, and developing a culture of trust with those around you.

> *In general, adults do not deliberately lie about their experiences. However, their experiences can differ significantly, as everyone views the world through their own unique lens. The question then becomes:*

where can these differing perspectives converge? Is it possible to find common ground and speak the same language? Ultimately, speaking the same language entails envisioning the future in a similar manner. Trust, after all, is rooted in the future. If we are not aligned in terms of what is possible in the future, if our visions diverge, it becomes challenging to establish mutual trust.

For instance, consider the Los Angeles teacher's union strikes (LAUSD, March 2023). The district may prioritize discussing vital matters, such as the cost of health benefits and budgetary balance. Meanwhile, the teachers' union may emphasize concerns surrounding the well-being of aging teachers and what would happen if they were to fall seriously ill. In order to move forward, both parties must engage in a shared conversation. They must envision a common future that fulfills their respective needs. Without the ability to imagine a future that accommodates the interests of all involved, repairing the relationship becomes exceedingly difficult. It is these very dynamics that can lead to relationship breakdowns, akin to why people opt for divorce.

Trust Me:
It's You

Developing Self-Trust

*"Trust: Choosing to risk making something you value vulnerable to another person's actions.
Distrust: What is important to me is not safe with the person in this situation (or any situation)."*
—Charles Feltman The Thin Book of Trust: An Essential Primer for Building Trust at Work[39]

Trust yourself.

That's easier said than done.

Emilee is a fifth-year fourth-grade teacher who loves her job, but she increasingly struggles to trust herself. Her third year of teaching was challenging. Faced with teaching hybrid virtual and in-person classes due to COVID lockdowns, she became unsettled and felt unsure of her abilities. She has always been confident in her teaching skills, but her third year shook her to the core. With all of the issues she and her students struggled through that year, after a while it was hard to keep believing that she was a good teacher in a broken system. Maybe she was just a poor teacher after all.

As she began her fourth year, Emilee constantly battled with the voices in her head. One voice would tell her she was a great teacher, she was knowledgeable and experienced, and her students loved her. Another voice, however, was less confident and less certain, but far louder. It reminded her of all the mistakes she had made, the times when she felt like she had failed her students, and the moments she doubted herself.

Emilee struggled to determine which voice to trust. Some days, she would feel confident and capable, but on others, she would be overcome with self-doubt. When she was preparing a lesson plan, one voice would tell her she had all the tools and resources she needed, while another voice would question her ability to execute the plan effectively. When she received positive feedback from a parent or student, one voice would tell her she was making a difference, but another would say it was just a fluke. Normal tasks she used to excel at began to trigger her and make her feel inexplicably useless.

The voices in our heads can be loud and persistent. Our internal dialogue can be ruthless and leave us withered, or cheer us on and inflate our egos. We often struggle to determine which voice to trust and which to distrust.

It's risky to trust, even to trust ourselves. What's the risk of trusting ourselves? What are we afraid will happen?

WE MIGHT BE AFRAID THAT:

- The voices in our heads are right...we are worthless, untrustworthy, stupid

- We will disappoint others or ourselves

- We will discover we're not who we wish we are...we're a poser

- We'll be hurt and taken advantage of

- Things will never turn out well for us, just as we suspected

- We'll find the proof that we don't make wise decisions

In his excellent book, *The Thin Book of Trust: An Essential Primer for Building Trust at Work*, Charles Feltman provides one of the best and most used definitions of trust and distrust. "Trust: Choosing to risk making something you value vulnerable to another person's actions. Distrust: What is important to me is not safe with the person in this situation (or any situation)." The problem is we don't just trust and distrust others. We trust and distrust ourselves.

So with some adjustments:

Trusting yourself is choosing to risk making something you value vulnerable to your own actions. And distrusting yourself is believing what is important to you is not safe with you in this situation (or any situation).

SELF-DISTRUST

Self-Distrust: What is important to you is not safe with you in this situation (or any situation).

The weight of that statement and its validity drives many to patterns of shame and depression. We've all experienced times when our actions don't match our values. We aren't our best selves, and tragic consequences often follow. We harbor the memories of these experiences, and our Guard Dog uses them to remind us how "dangerous" we are to ourselves. Our thoughts and actions are guided by:

- Dwelling on the past, the way "it's always been"

- Worrying about the future as if we can control it

- Letting knee-jerk emotions make decisions

- Perfectionism: no tolerance for feeling like a failure

- Procrastinating and breaking promises to ourselves

- Chronically looking to others for reassurance, instead of yourself

- Suppressing your curiosity in favor of what you "should be doing"[40]

Two years after the lock-downs, Emilee's voices haven't quieted. She replays specific incidents when she wasn't prepared during video class sessions. Out of anxiety about "doing things right," she puts off many tasks requested by her principal. The harder she tries to make a perfect lesson plan, the further she journeys away from connecting with her students. Emilee is convinced she'll be fired at the end of the year, and she's questioning her career decision.

When we allow our Guard Dog to turn against us, self-distrust can be debilitating, but that doesn't have to be the end of the story. As we've learned, all distrust isn't the same, and healthy distrust is necessary for trust to develop. The key to discovering how to use self-distrust to our benefit is to develop our relationship with our amygdala's Guard Dog and Guide Dog.

A Guard Dog shields you against dangerous situations. There are situations when our Guard Dog needs to bark warning signals to protect us from ourselves.

At one of her lowest points, Emilee began to skip her usual routine of going to the gym on her way home from work. Instead, she enjoyed a drive-through meal, stretched out on the couch watching the Hallmark Channel, and washed it all down with too many wine coolers. One morning, still on the couch with a slight hangover, the TV startled her awake and noticed she only had 10 minutes before needing to leave for work. She put on her makeup and drank a cup of strong coffee on the way, thankful the traffic was better than usual.

As she pulled into the shockingly empty school parking lot, she realized it was Saturday. All the way home she talked to herself in the rear-view mirror and committed to change. Even though her unhealthy habits were the result of the distrusting voices in her head, it was also her Guard Dog's loud bark that alerted her something had to change.

When we allow our Guard Dog to turn against us, self-distrust can be debilitating.

A healthy Guard Dog's bark is often needed to pull us back on track. We must learn how to notice the difference between a Guard Dog trying to protect us in ways that lead to guilt, shame, and poor performance, and a Guard Dog warning us about real danger in helpful ways. To build self-trust, it's crucial to start by becoming aware of the different influences of our internal Guard Dog.

What is important to us can sometimes become distorted. As Emilee's story illustrates, we can also think of distrust in a slightly different way: What had become important to her (the unhealthy defensive and depressive habits) was not safe for her in this situation (or any situation). Emilee's Guard Dog alerted her to pay attention to her own activities that weren't good for her. Our Guard Dog can warn us about danger coming from without and from within. Sometimes it is harder to believe that we could be harming ourselves.

We always have the option to transform our Guard Dog into a Guide Dog, which assists us in navigating dangers, rather than calling for a total shutdown. The amygdala's protective role remains, but now it acts as a guide. Rather than berating ourselves for a mistake, we give ourselves constructive criticism. Rather than doubting our abilities, we make a reasonable case for why we should or shouldn't try a new activity. During this stage, our Guide Dog leads us through curiosity-building questions, such as "What else could be true?" This question helps us explore other possibilities and determine if our own desires pose a threat to ourselves.

The move from Guard Dog to Guide Dog is the first phase of the Trust Flywheel. Trust development follows the same process, whether trusting others or ourselves. You must gain trust momentum in your own principles, abilities, and choices for sustainable self-trust. Again, trust is dynamic and not static. Practicing the elements of the Trust Flywheel accelerates the flywheel effect, which produces dependable self-trust.

SELF-TRUST

Self-trust: Choosing the risk of making something you value vulnerable to your own actions.

Emilee's car ride home was a turning point. After struggling with self-doubt for years, she resolved to regain self-trust. In the beginning of her career, she was confident in her actions and values. She wanted to be that self-assured person again. With her

Guard and Guide Dogs at the ready, she faced a choice: would she dare to put her values into action and help herself recover from the defensive habits she'd developed? Emilee was now entering the next stage of the Trust Flywheel: Engage Trust.

> "And that is the beautiful thing about trusting yourself to take new risks—it's where we can discover the most about ourselves. A lack of trust is what stops us exploring new directions and opportunities. It limits us."[41]

Trust doesn't just happen; it stems from acknowledging and overcoming distrust, and embracing the possibility of trust, especially self-trust. Self-trust is, first and foremost, a decision. It requires executive thought and reason. It demands taking a step, with the Guard Dog in one hand and the Guide Dog in the other, into uncertainty.

"Trusting yourself more means making the fear and doubts that come with uncertainty work for you."[42]

Learning to engage trust with ourselves is a fundamental step toward building self-confidence and achieving personal growth, but it can be challenging for those who have experienced trauma, self-doubt, or other negative experiences that have eroded their sense of self-trust. Self-trust is the courageous choice to face uncertainty and potential failure, and to take control of oneself. It leads to growth, improvement, and learning, even though it may not be comfortable or feel secure. Self-trust isn't a safe place, even though it emerges from a safe place. It thrives on adventure, ambiguity, and curiosity.

> Bren'e Brown suggests it takes "BRAVING" to obtain and maintain trust.
>
> "B – Did I respect my own **boundaries**? Was I clear about what's okay and what's not okay?
> R – Was I **reliable**? Did I do what I said I was going to do?
> A – Did I hold myself **accountable**?
> V – Did I respect the **vault** and share accordingly?
> I – Did I act from my **integrity**?
> N – Did I ask for what I **needed**? Was I non-judgmental about needing help?
> G – Was I **generous** towards myself?"[43]

"Courageous people aren't fearless. Far from it. They learn to make friends with uncertainty, to move through it, without it paralyzing them.[44]"

The first step towards engaging trust with oneself is self-awareness. This involves understanding yourself, including strengths, weaknesses, values, and goals. It also involves recognizing and addressing any negative self-talk or limiting beliefs that may be hindering your ability to trust yourself. By building self-awareness, you can begin to cultivate self-trust through self-care and self-compassion. Treat yourself with kindness and compassion, especially in the face of failure or setbacks. Set realistic goals and expectations and celebrate successes along the way. As self-trust is established, we can begin to take risks and try new things, strengthening our sense of self-trust.

SELF-TEST

Self-trust is fraught with ingredients that make a Guard Dog crazy. Mixing risk, ambiguity, failure, innovation, and learning is a recipe for Guard Dog Distrust. That doesn't sound like the positive outcome we expect when deciding to trust ourselves. Of course, we always hope not to deal with a barking dog again—at least not one that barks at us.

When we trust others and move into the last phase of the Trust Flywheel, Test Trust, it often surprises us. We might not expect a trusting relationship with another person to be tested so effortlessly. It's a different feeling when the time comes for testing trust in ourselves. Finding that we cannot trust our self might lead us to feel disappointment, defeat, and shame.

During summer break, Emilee started back at the gym. She took mindfulness and meditation classes and she made significant progress. She confidently entered her fourth-grade classroom the following year. Her inner dialogue was quiet and calm. Until...the cycle began again.

"It's not events from your past that make it hard to trust yourself—it's your habits in the present."[45]

All of us have had similar experiences. We begin to slip into old internal conversations about our worth. We feel like a poser, and it's hard to decide or know what to do. We're defeated again. How could we have ever thought anything different?

Handling the trust-testing phase properly is crucial for maintaining progress. It's a necessary step and can't be skipped. Trust will be challenged, including self-trust. We must mitigate the effects of our Guard Dog by encouraging it to move to a Guide Dog, not by attempting to shut the Dog up entirely. With the Guide Dog's help, we begin to trust at a different velocity, and the flywheel gains additional momentum. By reducing skepticism and transforming it into a supportive force, we can establish trust more deeply and give our progress additional momentum.

> No matter what the challenge, there are two things you can do when you find a lack of trust is holding you back:
>
> i. Do what you can to reduce the unknown.
>
> ii. Find the right people to have by your side to help build your confidence to sit and then [move] through the uncertainty.[46]

It is important to remain patient, persistent, and self-compassionate throughout this process and as we test our sense of self and self-trust. If there's one person you trust, make it yourself. Trusting oneself is the foundation for finding identity, significance, belonging, and hope. These fundamental life pursuits are only attainable with self-trust.

ONLY NOW ARE WE READY

Armed with a comprehensive understanding of the origins of broken self-trust and equipped with the knowledge of how to repair and rebuild it, we can move forward in strength. We can fully develop our individual and interpersonal trust toolboxes and purposefully mitigate distrust and engage the Trust Flywheel. Only now are we ready to take the first steps toward deliberately building a culture of trust, within and without.

> Distrust is a phenomenon that individuals experience without deliberate intent. Trust, on the other hand, requires conscious effort and intentionality. There are times when fatigue or weariness can contribute to a reluctance in cultivating trust. However, as educators, it remains crucial to actively mitigate distrust, even in situations where immediate trust may not be expected. It is important to acknowledge that the students being worked with might be tired and lacking energy, but it is still the responsibility of the educators to address and alleviate their distrust.

Consider the concept of resilience in this context. Resilience revolves around maintaining a continued sense of trust and belief, both in oneself and in others. If individuals lose confidence in their problem-solving abilities, trust in themselves diminishes, potentially leading them to give up. Similarly, if trust in the helpfulness of others wanes, it becomes challenging for individuals to rely on them. The question arises: How can these boundaries be bridged?

One powerful approach is the implementation of differentiated education. The goal of differentiation is to decrease self-distrust and foster self-confidence and self-efficacy in students. It involves recognizing that students can successfully tackle tasks at their personal level of readiness without diminishing the value or complexity of the content. By providing opportunities for success and gradually increasing the level of challenge, students experience an empowering sense of achievement. This process effectively lowers the barriers to distrust. Through ongoing exposure to trustworthy experiences, the flywheel of trust gains momentum. As students continually build upon their successes, they develop a greater sense of trust in themselves, the materials provided by the educational system, and the educators guiding them.

It is crucial to understand that lowering the barriers to distrust not only enhances individual self-confidence but also fosters an environment where students with limited reasons to trust can opt-in and engage more fully. By diminishing the obstacles that hinder trust, educators create an atmosphere that encourages students to actively participate and embrace the learning process.

By implementing differentiated education and providing ongoing trustworthy experiences, educators can help students develop self-confidence and self-efficacy. Lowering the barriers to distrust opens the door for students to engage more deeply and actively in their educational journey, fostering a positive and empowering learning environment.

Trust Me: We're In This Together

Building a Culture of Trust

> *"A trustworthy person and a trustworthy organization (culture) are not the same thing. It's perfectly possible to be a trustworthy person but fail to build a trustworthy organization (culture)."*[47]
> —David Horsager

Developing a culture of trust within an organization can have many benefits, such as increased collaboration and innovation, improved decision-making, and higher levels of employee engagement and satisfaction.

However, look around. Suspicion, name-calling, binary judgment, and snarky skepticism drive the current political, religious, and organizational cultures. Almost daily, I hear someone commenting on the state of "our world." It seems most, from all sides, are unhappy and wish it would change, yet hope for change is very low.

Why? We are struggling without the understanding that trust and distrust are autonomous processes. There's very little education about the amygdala, or how important acknowledging and addressing distrust is to the trust-building process. We cannot begin to build a trust culture until we shore up the foundations of our distrust and empower the healthy shift from Guard Dog to Guide Dog.

So, how do we make our way through the muck and mire to discover, uncover, and develop a trust culture? By understanding and working with the Trust Flywheel.

It's simple—build a trust account and get rid of the distrust, right?

Leaders anxiously twist themselves into knots trying to eliminate distrust and encourage a trust culture. "Most people think of trust like a bank account...you honor some commitments, you help people out, you tell the truth, and you think that you are putting trust, like money, into that account," writes David Horsager. "You think that it sits there waiting for you when you need it. But that's not how it works. If you don't continually reinforce trust in any relationship it will erode and disappear, no matter how much was in your bank account last week, last month, last year."[48] Trust isn't static. Trust is dynamic and it never just sits in an account waiting to be used.

In an effort to build a trust account, leaders offer fad-of-the-moment solutions like ping-pong and foosball tables, nap stations, and board games in the café. And it's no wonder. "Compared with people at low-trust companies, people at high-trust companies report 74% less stress, 106% more energy at work, 50% higher productivity, 13% fewer sick days, 76% more engagement, 29% more satisfaction with their lives, 40% less burnout."[49] In a PwC report, 55% of CEOs indicate that a lack of trust is a threat to their organization's growth.[50] Leaders grasp at anything that promises to build trust and diminish distrust. Yet, because trust must be continually replenished, many leaders are exhausted by their efforts to keep their trust bank account full, and are often confused when trust gestures from the past don't sustain trust indefinitely.

The truth is, trust develops. Momentum builds with the push-pull interaction between trust and distrust. It's much like the potential and kinetic energy exchange when swinging on a playground. Swings work by converting potential energy into kinetic energy, then kinetic energy back into potential energy, over and over again. As you fling your legs forward you pull back with your arms to advance, and then at the apex, you transfer to the opposite position and push forward with your arms and back with your legs. Each peak stores potential energy and it's transferred into speed, kinetic energy, and then potential energy again. The higher you go on the swing, the more potential energy you have.

Distrust is "potential energy" for the "kinetic energy" of trust. They push and pull on one another to provide trust momentum.

Thus, when forming a good definition of a trust culture, both trust and distrust must be included. Our definition is:

A CULTURE OF TRUST IS ONE IN WHICH INDIVIDUALS ARE SAFE TO BOTH APPROPRIATELY TRUST AND APPROPRIATELY DISTRUST.

As you may expect by now, when we research current mainstream definitions for "culture of trust," we find a very imbalanced perspective. We find lists of behaviors like transparency, accountability, consistency, and dependability being advertised as elixirs for trust. Each behavior villainizes distrust and focuses on ignoring or eliminating it. The message is simple: "Practice each of these behaviors, and you'll eventually eliminate distrust—therefore, producing a culture of trust."

> Here are some steps you can take to cultivate a culture of trust within your organization:
>
> • **Communicate openly and transparently**: Make sure that information is shared openly and honestly within your organization, and that there is transparency in decision-making processes.
> • **Practice accountability**: Hold yourself and others accountable for their actions and for their follow-through on commitments.
> • **Foster mutual respect**: Treat others with respect and kindness, and encourage others to do the same.
> • **Be reliable**: Follow through on your commitments and fulfill your responsibilities.
> • **Build trust through actions**: Actions speak louder than words, so make sure your actions align with your words and you are consistently reliable and trustworthy.
> • **Encourage open communication**: Encourage employees to share their ideas and feedback openly, and create a safe space for employees to speak up without fear of retribution.
> • **Foster a positive work environment**: Create a work environment that is positive, inclusive, and supportive, and make sure employees feel valued and supported.
> By taking these steps and consistently demonstrating trustworthiness, you can create a culture of trust within your organization.[51]

As we've already discussed, the absence of distrust doesn't necessarily develop trust. Remember, trust and distrust are processed in different areas of the brain. They are separate concepts.

When seeking to design a culture of trust, there are specific tools to mitigate distrust AND a different set of tools to develop trust. Useful tools used for the wrong purpose may fool us into thinking we're accomplishing our goals.

The Trust Flywheel framework provides the momentum necessary for a trust culture. It also requires the implementation of different tool sets during each stage: mitigate distrust, engage trust, and test trust. Understanding when to apply each tool set generates increased energy and allows trust momentum to evolve.

THE ONGOING PROCESS TO DEVELOPING A CULTURE OF TRUST IS:

- Recognize the Trust Flywheel stage you're currently in

- Access the appropriate tool set

- Repeat as the Flywheel turns and gains momentum

Trust is not static and requires momentum to sustain a culture. Just like repeating the process used to continue swinging at the park, you must continually repeat the process to continue developing and maintaining a trust culture.

DOG TOYS, INQUIRIES, AND SELF-LEADERSHIP

How do we determine which tools are for each Trust Flywheel stage?

The first stage is mitigating distrust. The tools vital during the mitigate distrust phase will:

- Create an environment where a Guard Dog is encouraged to move to a Guide Dog

- Mitigate Guard Dog triggers and boost social interaction standards

- Generate a calm and safe space for the decision to trust

- Focus on behaviors that motivate psychological and physical safety.

Interestingly enough, the lists of behaviors touted by mainstream trends as tools for building trust, like transparency, accountability, consistency, and dependability, all qualify to mitigate distrust. These behaviors are designed to diminish Guard Dog triggers and, when applied, whistle the Guide Dog into action. They promote a secure environment by reinforcing a reliable routine. Each provides standards for social interaction, and even though they don't necessarily increase the level of trust, they provide a base where a decision to trust can easily be achieved.

> "A culture of distrust can be created in many ways, including:
>
> • Lack of transparency: If information is not shared openly and honestly, it can create suspicion and mistrust.
> • Lack of accountability: If there is a lack of accountability, it can create a perception that people are not being held accountable for their actions.
> • Lack of respect: If there is a lack of mutual respect among employees and leaders, it can lead to a lack of trust.
> • Lack of reliability: If people are not reliable or do not follow through on their commitments, it can lead to a lack of trust.
> • Negative work environment: A negative or toxic work environment can also contribute to a culture of distrust.
> • Unfair treatment: If employees feel that they are being treated unfairly, it can lead to a lack of trust in the organization.
> • Poor communication: If there is poor communication within the organization, it can lead to misunderstandings and mistrust.
>
> By creating a culture that lacks transparency, accountability, respect, reliability, and positive communication, an organization can foster a culture of distrust."[52]

Transparency, accountability, consistency, and dependability are only components of the first step. If these are the only tools used, lowering the level of distrust may be accomplished, but trust development is ignored. And yet, a culture that lacks these nurtures Guard Dog Distrust, ergo heightening the levels of distrust and eroding the environment where trust can grow. Transparency, accountability, consistency, and dependability are necessary to get the Trust Flywheel moving.

Let's take a quick look at each tool for mitigating distrust, and extend its application within the trust ecosystem.

TRANSPARENCY

Transparency and accountability became vogue in the early 2000s as an onslaught of failed businesses, religious organizations, and government officials replenished the news cycle. Enron acts as the poster child for these collapses and their causes. New rules and regulations, standards and expectations, and a barking Guard Dog Distrust championed transparency and accountability.

Why is transparency so coveted? Transparency answers the warning bark: "I don't trust you to tell me what I need to know to be safe in this relationship." There is safety in knowing. Transparency is an effort to shine a light on the unknown darkness, and we hope that in knowing it all, we will be safe. However, trust isn't concerned with safety. The amygdala processes safety, thus, connecting it with distrust. Our need for safety is a need to calm the amygdala and mitigate distrust. Safety (transparency) doesn't develop trust; it mitigates distrust. Again, it's necessary, but in and of itself, it can't build a culture of trust.

Transparency has two key elements to consider:

- Full transparency eliminates the need for trust. If you are completely aware of the situation or you know everything, there's no need for trust. Trust requires the presence of the unknown. Complete transparency doesn't develop a culture of trust because it eliminates the unknown; thus, there's no need for trust.

- Total and complete transparency is a fallacy...and should be. Every relationship and every team has a transparency threshold. There's a limit to how much transparency is helpful and healthy. If the President of the United States were completely transparent at every moment, it would create havoc and panic. The same is true inside an organization, a team, and a classroom. Managing the transparency threshold is critical to developing a Guide Dog Distrust that moves the Trust Flywheel.

This threshold can be defined by three variables

1. The current level of transparency: How much are you telling me right now, and how much can I handle you telling me?

2. The transparency line of credit: The extra stuff you COULD tell me without negatively impacting our overall trust by triggering Guard Dog Distrust

3. The transparency threshold: this is the limit of transparency, beyond which our trust will be negatively impacted

In order to leverage the Transparency Threshold to mitigate distrust, it is important to be keenly aware of the proximity the information being shared is to that threshold. Stepping over the line can immediately trigger Guard Dogs and increase or cement distrust.

Everyone in the room was excited and looking forward to hearing the latest updates from Mark. Mark is the beloved CEO and trusted friend of most in the room. This update was particularly interesting as everyone knew that the company intended to make some broad strategic adjustments. As Mark made his way through his presentation, the anticipation increased. He masterfully reminded everyone of the history and growth accomplished. The announcement couldn't have landed better. The adjustments would likely improve everyone's quality of life. Curated details were carefully shared. The impending celebration was close at hand, and then Mark made a crucial error. He crossed the transparency threshold.

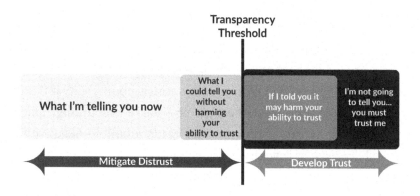

Mark began to share what the company and each relationship in the room meant to him and his family. Warm moments littered his personal confession until he mentioned that the company had provided for his family in abundance and had put him in a position of not having to work any longer. This information was all technically true and delivered in the 'spirit of transparency,' but there was an immediate and distinct change in the room's atmosphere. That one piece of information called Mark's motives into question. It was almost possible to hear people's internal questions. Did he design the details and decision to make the changes for the good of the company and everyone in the room? Or was it for his personal gain?

Describing how the company had provided for his family was perfectly placed as he walked up to the transparency threshold. However, he crossed it by sharing that he was so well off because of these organizational adjustments that he no longer had to work.

Transparency has the power to mitigate distrust and, when utilized beyond the threshold of the group, can produce a Guard Dog Distrust. Transparency may influence distrust, but it can't produce trust.

ACCOUNTABILITY

"Fewer words in corporate vernacular induce a tighter wince than 'accountability,' and for good reason. Companies and leaders have grappled with what it is and how to achieve it effectively for decades."[53] "The fundamental problem with accountability is that it now involves little more than the process of accounting. The scorekeeping nature of this process yields a built-in negativity bias, where leaders reflexively hunt for shortfalls, and the tallying usually ends with a forced categorization—a rating system of numbers or labels, sometimes stack-ranking employees against their peers." [54]

The etymology of "accountability" provides some insight into why the word brings on gnashing of teeth. At first glance, its roots mean nothing more than "to count." However, a closer look at its history reveals two distinct concepts that could make us cringe. So what is the historical meaning? "Liable to be called to account."[55] It sounds like being summoned before the judge and jury. The concepts of liability and "to give an answer for", combine for a system where "keeping record of wrongs" encourages judgment, shame, disappointment, insignificance, and low self-worth. If these are the possible results, why do we seek them?

Accountability can mitigate the warning bark: "I don't trust you to think for yourself, ask the right questions, to answer with accurate information, and or operate independently for the good of the team or relationship." Thus, the need to "count" or keep records of the process, incremental achievements, GAP analysis, victories, and failures. When the accumulation of these assessments is synthesized and recorded numerically, we may feel threatened. The search for significance, identity, belonging, and hope fall under attack, or at least are questioned when we are categorically evaluated. And where is the threat processed in the brain? The amygdala.

> **THREATENED BY ACCOUNTABILITY**
> A recent neuroscientific study revealed that we respond to being categorically rated with a sense of being threatened—we literally feel unsafe when someone puts us in a box in this way.[56]

Our intention isn't to create a threat but instead to mitigate the distrust between an organization and those providing services. So, how do we mitigate both the threat and distrust? Ron Carucci suggests[57] three elements that, when mixed with accountability, move Guard Dog to Guide Dog and ease the threat.

He recommends stirring in:

- Dignity

- Fairness

- Restoration

> "Our accountability systems have painfully confused sameness with fairness and have been designed largely to avoid litigation and reduce a manager's biases. In practice, they've done more to stunt individuality, and that's exactly what makes them unfair."[58]

Accountability triggers the amygdala and, ergo, distrust. It's essential to create systems where dignity, fairness, and restoration guide our need to force someone to give an account. Yet, this mixture doesn't provide the entire recipe for a trust culture.

CONSISTENCY/DEPENDABILITY

We enjoy the security of someone we can count on—they are a warm blanket in a cold world of uncertainty. The more consistent and dependable they are, the easier it is to decide to trust. While consistency and dependability may be critical elements in trustworthiness and support the decision to trust, they do not develop a culture of trust by themselves.[59] They lower or mitigate distrust.

> *"Being dependable and maintaining reliability is the fourth element of trustworthiness. One of the quickest ways people erode trust is by not following through on commitments. Conversely, those who do what they say they are going to do earn a reputation of being consistent and trustworthy."*[60]

This is more easily seen if we review it from the other side. When a person breaks dependability and isn't consistent in their performance, a greater need to distrust emerges, not necessarily a lowering of trust. Consistency and dependability answer the warning bark: "I don't trust you to fail or handle failure in a way that fosters or delivers ingenuity, invention, innovation, and future competency."

> *"Consistency. The final element of trust is the extent to which leaders walk their talk and do what they say they will do. People rate a leader high in trust if they:*
> * *Are a role model and set a good example.*
> * *Walk the talk.*

> • Honor commitments and keep promises.
> • Follow through on commitments.
> • Are willing to go above and beyond what needs to be done."[61]

Consistency and dependability are performance-based analyses. I'm not seen as trustworthy if I consistently fail at what I do. We view consistency and dependability from a positive performance position. It's only when I consistently and dependably succeed that I'm deemed trustworthy. Because we hold this bias, consistency and dependability are tools to keep the Guard Dog at bay and allow the Guide Dog to support the decision to trust.

Transparency, accountability, consistency, and dependability can lower or mitigate distrust. They aid in moving Guard Dog to Guide Dog and therefore, they are essential to get the Trust Flywheel moving. Keeping the momentum requires a new set of tools. These tools encourage decision-making, executive thought, and reason. They engage the prefrontal cortex.

UNLIKELY SUSPECTS THAT DEVELOP A TRUST CULTURE

If you're thinking, "now what?" you're not alone. It seems that all the mainstream trust-building tools start the Trust Flywheel turning, but are anemic when sustaining the momentum necessary to develop a trust culture. A trust culture is developed as the Trust Flywheel gains momentum. Moving from mitigating distrust, the second stage of the Trust Flywheel is to engage trust. The key is to employ the prefrontal cortex when seeking to make a decision to trust.

It may seem counterintuitive, but ambiguity, the presence of "why," agency, and a safe place to fail are tools that engage the decision to trust. Each of these stimulates the prefrontal cortex to begin its work. One organization that has employed the push and pull of distrust and trust is Spotify.

Spotify streams music, videos, and podcasts to over 30 million paying subscribers. With $3 billion in revenue and 2,000+ employees organized into agile, self-organizing, cross-functional squads, Spotify has succeeded in maintaining dexterity and agency without sacrificing accountability and transparency. It enables innovation while keeping the benefits of dependability, and it creates alignment with employee agency.

> *"Spotify's core organizational unit is an autonomous squad of no more than eight people. Each squad is accountable for a discrete aspect of the product, which it owns cradle to grave. Squads have the authority to decide what to build, how to build it, and with whom to work to make the product interoperable. They are organized into a light matrix called a tribe. Tribes comprise several squads linked together through a chapter, which is a horizontal grouping that helps to support specific competencies such as quality assistance, agile coaching, and web development. The chapter's primary role is to facilitate learning and competency development throughout the squads.*
>
> *Leadership within the squad is self-determined, while the chapter leader is a formal manager who focuses on coaching and mentoring. Spotify believes in the player-coach model: Chapter leaders are also squad members. Squad members can switch squads and retain the same formal leader within their chapter. Spotify introduced a third organizational element, known as a guild. Guilds are lightweight communities of interest whose primary purpose is to share knowledge in areas that cut across chapters and squads, such as leadership, continuous delivery, and web delivery.*
>
> *This unusual combination of squads, tribes, chapters, and guilds is the organizational infrastructure that underlies Spotify's operating model. At first reading, it might sound like just another way to define a conventional organizational matrix in Millennial- and digital-friendly terms. But a closer examination reveals just how different the model really is and why it seems to work so well."*[62]

Spotify's squads are autonomous, and while they are responsible for their projects from birth to grave, there is a unique, self-directed system for accountability. Squads go through postmortem analysis and are required to understand both success and failure. "Fail Walls" are scattered throughout the workplace, where failures are posted, allowing others to learn and to honor failing fast. Squads also don't have prescribed leaders. Leadership emerges organically and shifts informally as the project moves through its lifecycle. Displaying failures without judgment allows Guard Dog Distrust to move to Guide Dog, and honoring fast failure engages executive thought learning, ergo, developing trust. Mixing agentic accountability and autonomy is a great path to build momentum and develop trust through the Trust Flywheel.

Once you've taken steps to mitigate distrust in a relationship, it's important to look out for signs that it's time to move on to developing trust. You may find that you can communicate more openly and honestly in the relationship without feeling judged or criticized. Mitigating distrust through consistency is also an important factor to consider. If your partner's or colleague's behavior is consistent over time, and you feel like you can rely on them, this is a good sign that you can start deciding to trust. When the other person takes responsibility after a previous trust breakdown, it can empower you to get the Trust Flywheel moving again. And, of course, mutual respect and willingness to put in the effort to take trust leaps contribute to that momentum.

Using each of the mainstream "trust-building" tools as launchpads for mitigating distrust, we can make the pivot to the tools that actually help develop trust.

MOVING FROM TRANSPARENCY TO AMBIGUITY

Ambiguity can be a powerful tool for building trust in any relationship, be it personal or professional. When there is a lack of clear information, people can easily jump to conclusions or make assumptions. However, when ambiguity is used intentionally and thoughtfully, it can foster trust by encouraging open communication and collaboration. Open, collaborative communication engages the prefrontal cortex.

One way that ambiguity develops trust is by leaving room for interpretation. This allows for multiple perspectives and encourages people to share their thoughts and ideas. When everyone feels heard and valued, it creates a sense of mutual respect and understanding. This, in turn, creates an environment where people feel comfortable sharing information and being open about their needs, which is key to developing trust.

> "Facing highly ambiguous challenges will help managers develop a set of tools that prepare them for the uncertainties they will increasingly encounter as they ascend up the corporate ladder."[63]
>
> "Shifting from size-matters to ambiguity-matters development requires rethinking other key assumptions. Most companies, for example, look to what a manager has achieved to assess their performance. But in ambiguous circumstances with uncertain outcomes, you need to look at how a manager has acted. Sometimes you can do everything right and forces beyond your control lead to 'failure'."[64]

Another way that ambiguity develops trust is by creating a sense of shared ownership. When people are given the space to interpret information and share their perspectives, they become more invested in the outcome. This creates a sense of shared responsibility and a willingness to work together to find a solution. When people feel that they are working toward a common goal, they are more likely to trust each other and collaborate effectively.

Finally, ambiguity can help to develop trust by fostering a sense of vulnerability. When people are not given all the information, they are forced to be more open and honest about what they do and do not know. This creates a sense of vulnerability that encourages people to be more open and honest with each other. This vulnerability, in turn, creates a sense of empathy and understanding, which are crucial components of trust development. In this way, ambiguity can be a powerful tool for developing trust in any relationship.

> "Ultimately, trust is the biggest competitive advantage any organization can possess because it's what keeps people coming back for more—whether its employees or customers."[65]

MOVING FROM ACCOUNTABILITY TO "WHY?"

The presence and use of "why" can develop momentum as we decide to trust. Asking "why" encourages people to think critically and understand the reasoning behind a particular decision or action. This helps to develop trust as it opens the prefrontal cortex to reason.

> "High-trust organizations understand that trust is valuable and are therefore restlessly committed to communicating the 'why' behind decisions. High-trust organizations know that's how they create clarity and gain buy-in. High-trust organizations refuse to leave people second-guessing."[66]

The presence and use of "why" can also help to build trust by promoting shared and collaborative reasoning. When people understand the reasoning behind a decision or action, they are more likely to trust that it was made for the right reasons. And when a person can share a reason behind their own thoughts and actions, the momentum to trust is increased. By asking "why," people are encouraged to think critically and understand the reasoning behind a particular decision or action, which in turn helps to develop trust.

MOVING FROM CONSISTENCY TO AGENCY

Giving a person agency refers to empowering them to make decisions and take actions that affect their own lives. This can be done by providing them with the necessary resources, information, and support to make informed choices. Giving a person agency can help to develop trust by fostering a sense of autonomy, responsibility, and empowerment.

When a person is given agency, they are empowered to make decisions that affect their own lives. This can include decisions related to their health, education, and financial well-being. By giving a person agency, they can take control of their own lives and make choices that align with their own values and goals. This sense of autonomy and self-determination can help to develop trust by giving the person a sense of ownership over their own life.

Giving a person agency also promotes a sense of responsibility. When a person is empowered to make decisions and take action, they are also responsible for the outcomes of those decisions and actions. This can help develop trust by showing that the person can make responsible choices and be accountable for their actions' consequences. This agentic accountability requires the prefrontal cortex to engage and promotes the decision to trust. Lastly, giving a person agency can foster a sense of empowerment. When a person is empowered to make decisions and take action, they can see the direct impact of their choices and actions on their own lives. This can help develop trust by showing that the person can make meaningful changes in their own lives and that they have the power to shape their own future. Additionally, by giving agency, we are showing trust in the person's ability to make good decisions, which may foster a reciprocal effect.

> ## "HIGH-TRUST ORGANIZATIONS ARE BRILLIANT AT MAKING EMPLOYEES FEEL SEEN."[67]

Giving a person agency can develop trust by fostering a sense of autonomy, responsibility, and empowerment, by allowing them to make decisions and take actions that affect their own lives, and by showing that they are capable of making responsible choices and being accountable for the consequences of their actions.

MOVING FROM DEPENDABILITY TO FAILING FAST

A culture that allows for "failing fast" can help develop trust by promoting a culture of experimentation, learning, and innovation. This type of culture encourages teams to take risks, try new things, and learn from their failures, which can lead to greater creativity, collaboration, and, ultimately, success. All of these activities are processed in the prefrontal cortex and promote the decision to trust.

People are more likely to take chances and try new approaches by providing a safe environment where failure is not punished but instead is seen as an opportunity to learn. This can lead to greater creativity and experimentation, which can ultimately result in innovative solutions and new opportunities. They learn to trust themselves, those leading them, and the organization.

When people are encouraged to learn from their failures, they are more likely to identify areas for improvement and take steps to address them. This can lead to a more resilient and adaptable organization, which can ultimately result in greater success and momentum to trust. Additionally, allowing failure to happen fast without shame means that organizations can quickly pivot, adjust, and move forward, which can also be seen as a sign of trust in their employees and their ability to learn and adapt.

The Trust Tested phase of the Trust Flywheel is where the concept of fast failure comes into play. In order to build a culture of trust, it's important to prioritize taking risks and trying new things, even if failure is a possibility. A culture of dependability can sometimes stifle creativity and innovation, leading to a lack of growth and progress. By testing trust and embracing the possibility of failure, individuals and teams can learn from their mistakes and develop a culture of trust that values risk-taking, learning, and growth.

> "Most executive teams engage in annual strategic planning sessions focused on improving their business the following year, but trust is rarely on the agenda. It's a shame, because in many cases, the key to success lies not in creating an entirely new strategy, but in dismantling barriers to trust within a given organization."[68]

This third and final momentum-generator on the Trust Flywheel might come as a surprise to people who have been educated by the hyper-positivity of mainstream trust culture dynamics. Instead of trying to avoid every scenario where someone might challenge the trust in our relationship, we should anticipate that phase, and empower ourselves to keep the trust momentum going through the discomfort.

Recognizing when a student is testing the trust in the relationship can be challenging. Still, some signs to watch for include a decrease in communication or engagement, pushback against feedback or guidance, and increased defensiveness or avoidance. To help the relationship make it through this phase, it is important to practice active listening and empathetic understanding. Teachers can use relationship tools like reflective listening, positive reinforcement, and non-judgmental communication to foster open and honest dialogue with their students.

It is important to watch for signs of burnout and compassion fatigue in yourself, such as emotional exhaustion or decreased motivation. In the student's behavior, watch for signs of stress, anxiety, or depression, such as withdrawal, poor academic performance, or changes in behavior. To respond to a student testing trust in a productive and healthy way, teachers should remain calm and patient, acknowledge the student's concerns and feelings, and work collaboratively with the student to identify solutions and build trust. This can involve setting clear boundaries and expectations, providing consistent and fair feedback, and offering support and resources as needed. Ultimately, it is important to approach the situation with a growth mindset and a willingness to learn and adapt to strengthen the relationship and support the student's growth and development.

When a trust breakdown occurs, it is important to address the issue head-on to move toward the "mitigate distrust" phase and keep the Trust Flywheel moving. One of the best ways to handle a trust breakdown is to communicate openly and honestly with the other person. This involves acknowledging any mistakes or missteps, apologizing for any harm caused, and taking responsibility for actions or decisions that may have contributed to the breakdown. It also involves actively listening to the other person's perspective and concerns, and working collaboratively to identify and address any underlying issues.

Another key element of moving from the "test trust" phase to the "mitigate distrust" phase is to set clear expectations and boundaries. This might involve establishing guidelines for communication or behavior, defining roles and responsibilities, or developing a shared understanding of goals and objectives. By setting clear expectations and boundaries, individuals can create a sense of stability and predictability, which can help to build trust over time. Additionally, seeking outside help or support, such as through therapy or mediation, can be a helpful tool in mitigating distrust and rebuilding trust in a relationship.

WHAT CAN STOP ME NOW?

With the tools to mitigate distrust and develop trust, the possibilities for relationships are endless. By actively taking steps to repair and rebuild trust, individuals can create a strong foundation for healthy and productive connections. When equipped with these tools, we can confidently navigate potential obstacles and challenges that may arise in our relationships.

We no longer have to feel limited by past distrust or the fear of vulnerability. By engaging in open communication, setting clear boundaries and expectations, and working collaboratively to overcome challenges, we can create a culture of trust and mutual support. This culture can extend beyond our personal relationships to our professional lives as well, allowing us to thrive in all aspects of our lives.

So, what can stop us now? With the power of distrust and trust, we can overcome even the most difficult obstacles and achieve success in our personal and professional lives. It all starts with taking intentional steps to mitigrate distrust, build trust, and test trust. By doing so, we can unlock the full potential of our relationships.

The conversation surrounding different grading protocols and methods can be viewed as an opportunity to lower the thresholds for distrust in the classroom. Disturbingly, research reveals that within the first 10 to 14 school days, when teachers are asked to predict students' graded outcomes, their initial perceptions often correlate with the actual grade outcomes. This unfortunate pattern means that teachers have already formed preconceived notions about students' capabilities and have categorized them, whether consciously or unconsciously. Students are highly perceptive and can sense when they are being labeled or predicted in such a way, which can shape their experience within the classroom environment.

However, by implementing alternative grading methods, it becomes possible to reduce the barriers to trust. In a recent example from Clark County, students were asked to prioritize their concerns, and it is intriguing that their top priorities at the end of the school year mirrored those at the beginning. Their foremost concern is increased safety within schools, as they often feel a sense of insecurity and fear the possibility of harm. They are also genuinely concerned about their mental health and that of their peers, recognizing the impact of anxiety, fear, and depression on their overall well-being. Lastly, students expressed a desire for more engaged and caring teachers. It is important to recognize that all three of these priorities are foundational to building trust within the classroom environment.

A thought-provoking phrase that encapsulates this concept is, "I had to Maslow before I could Bloom." Abraham Maslow's hierarchy of needs emphasizes that individuals must trust that their essential needs will be met before they can fully engage in higher cognitive needs, as represented by Benjamin Bloom. Trusting that their basic needs for safety, security, and well-being will be addressed allows students to focus on their academic and personal growth. By addressing these fundamental concerns and fostering an environment where students feel safe, supported, and cared for, educators can create a solid foundation of trust that enables students to thrive academically and emotionally.

Appendix

Enneagram	Myers-Briggs	Motivational Resource that Encourages the Speed of Trust	Motivational Resource that Encourages the Speed of Distrust
1 The Reformer	ISTJ, INTJ (ITJ)	· To be good, to have integrity, to be balanced · Improve · Ideals	· Corrupt/evil · Defective
2 The Helper	ESFJ, ENFJ (EF)	· To feel loved · Express their feelings · To be needed and appreciated	· Being unwanted, unworthy of being loved
3 The Achiever	ESTJ, ENTJ (ETJ)	· To feel valuable and worthwhile · Affirmed, to distinguish themselves from others, to have attention, to be admired, and to impress others.	· Being worthless

Enneagram	Myers-Briggs	Motivational Resource that Encourages the Speed of Trust	Motivational Resource that Encourages the Speed of Distrust
4 The Individualist	INFP, INFJ (INF)	· Find themselves and their significance (to create an identity) · Express themselves and their individuality, to create and surround themselves with beauty, to maintain certain moods and feelings, to withdraw to protect their self-image, to take care of emotional needs before attending to anything else, to attract a "rescuer."	· No identity or personal significance
5 The Investigator	INTP, INTJ (INT)	· Capable and competent · Possess knowledge, to understand the environment, to have everything figured out as a way of defending the self from threats from the environment	· Being useless, helpless, or incapable
6 The Loyalist	ISFJ, ISTJ (ISJ)	· Security and support · Certitude and reassurance, to test the attitudes of others toward them, to fight against anxiety and insecurity	· Being without support and guidance

Enneagram	Myers-Briggs	Motivational Resource that Encourages the Speed of Trust	Motivational Resource that Encourages the Speed of Distrust
7 The Enthusiast	ENFP, ENTP (ENP)	· Satisfied and content—to have their needs fulfilled · Maintain their freedom and happiness, to avoid missing out on worthwhile experiences, to keep themselves excited and occupied, to avoid and discharge pain	· Deprived and in pain
8 The Challenger	ESTJ, ENTJ (ETJ)	· To protect themselves (to be in control of their own life and destiny) · Self-reliant, to prove their strength and resist weakness, to be important in their world, to dominate the environment, and to stay in control of their situation.	· Being harmed or controlled by others
9 The Peacemaker	ISFP, ISFJ (ISF)	· Inner stability and "peace of mind" · Create harmony in their environment, to avoid conflicts and tension, to preserve things as they are, to resist whatever would upset or disturb them	· Loss and separation

Endnotes

1   The outcome produced my first two books: *The Search to Belong* (Zondervan) and *Organic Community* (Baker).
2   The term Fourth Estate or fourth power refers to the press and news media both in explicit capacity of advocacy and implicit ability to frame political issues.
3   Botsman, Rachel. Who Can You Trust?: How Technology Brought Us Together -- and Why It Could Drive US Apart. Penguin Business, 2018.
4   IBID.
5   Botsman, Rachel. "Why Trust Matters with Rachel Botsman Online Class: Linkedin Learning, Formerly Lynda.Com." LinkedIn, www.linkedin.com/learning/why-trust-matters-with-rachel-botsman. Accessed 14 Mar. 2020.
6   SoP. "Amygdala." The Science of Psychotherapy, 1 Oct. 2018, www.thescienceofpsychotherapy.com/glossary/amygdala/.
7   Sturm, Mike. "Rachel Botsman: An Economy of Trust." Nordic Business Forum, 4 Feb. 2018, www.nbforum.com/nbreport/rachel-botsman-economy-trust/.
8   Fitzgerald, Chantelle. "The Anatomy of Trust: By Bren'e Brown." LinkedIn, 14 Dec. 2015, www.linkedin.com/pulse/anatomy-trust-brene-brown-chantelle-fitzgerald.
9   User Clip: Doveryai, No Proveryai: Trust but Verify." C-span, www.c-span.org/video/?c4694150%2Fdoveryai-proveryai-trust-verify. Accessed 16 May 2023.
10   Meyer, Pamela M. Liespotting: Proven Techniques to Detect Deception. St. Martin's Press, 2017.
11   IBID.
12   "2017 Edelman Trust Barometer." Edelman, 2017, www.edelman.com/trust/2017-trust-barometer. The Trust Index is an average of a country's trust in the institutions of government, business, media, and NGOs. Informed Public and Mass Population, 28-country global total.
13   "Sharp Partisan Divisions in Views of National Institutions." Pew Research Center - U.S. Politics & Policy, 10 July 2017, www.pewresearch.org/politics/2017/07/10/sharp-partisan-divisions-in-views-of-national-institutions/.
14   Kennedy, Brian. "Most Americans Trust the Military and Scientists to Act in the Public's Interest." Pew Research Center, 18 Oct. 2016, www.pewresearch.org/short-reads/2016/10/18/most-americans-trust-the-military-and-scientists-to-act-in-the-publics-interest/.
15   Botsman, Rachel. Who Can You Trust? How Technology Brought Us Together and Why It Might Drive Us Apart. Public Affairs, 2018.
16   The History of Matchmaking Around the World: Single Atlanta." Atlanta Matchmaking Service, atlantamatchmakers.com/blog/history-of-matchmaking. Accessed 22 May 2023.
17   "The Art of Matchmaking in Japan, Korea, and China." Psychology Today, www.psychologytoday.com/us/blog/culture-shocked/201609/the-art-matchmaking-in-japan-korea-and-china. Accessed 22 May 2023.
18   "The Memetic Tribes of Culture War 2.0." Medium, 21 Aug. 2020, medium.com/s/world-wide-wtf/memetic-tribes-and-culture-war-2-0-14705c43f6bb.

19   Cortisol is released when Guard Dog Distrust is activated. Cortisol shuts down logical-processing thought. During a risk-stressed event logical-processing thought is inaccessible primarily because it's too slow to react to an environment that requires safety.
20   "What Are Microexpressions?" Humintell.Com, www.humintell.com/microexpressions-2/. Accessed 22 May 2023.
21   Willis, J., and A. Todorov. "First Impressions: Making up Your Mind after a 100-MS Exposure to a Face." Psychological Science, 17 July 2006, pubmed.ncbi.nlm.nih.gov/16866745/.
22   Mujica-Parodi, Lilianne R., et al. "Chemosensory Cues to Conspecific Emotional Stress Activate Amygdala in Humans." PLoS ONE, vol. 4, no. 7, 2009, https://doi.org/10.1371/journal.pone.0006415.
23   (Author),   . "What Makes a Voice Trustworthy?"   I   , bayanebartar.org/trustworthy-voice. Accessed 22 May 2023.
24   (and family) - author's addition.
25   Porath, Christine Lynne. Mastering Civility: A Manifesto for the Workplace. Grand Central Publishing, 2016.
26   Galef, Julia. "The Scout Mindset: Why Some People See Things Clearly And Others Don't" 2021.
27   Botsman, Rachel. Who Can You Trust? How Technology Brought Us Together and Why It Might Drive Us Apart. Public Affairs, 2018.
28   February 6, 2019. "Are You Being Manipulated?" Seth's Blog, 17 Dec. 2020, seths.blog/2019/02/are-you-being-manipulated/.
29   Communications, NYU Web. "Psychologists Find Unintentional Racial Biases May Affect Economic and Trust Decisions." NYU, 25 Apr. 2011, www.nyu.edu/about/news-publications/news/2011/april/psychologists-find-unintentional-racial-biases-may-affect-economic-trust-decisions.html.
30   Lewicki, Roy J., et al. "Trust and Distrust: New Relationships and Realities." Academy of Management Review, vol. 23, no. 3, July 1998, pp. 438–458, https://doi.org/10.5465/amr.1998.926620.
31   Alvin Gouldner, 1955114 Williams NR. How to get a 2:1 in media, communication and cultural studies. London: Sage; 2004.
32   "Momentum." The Physics Classroom, www.physicsclassroom.com/Class/momentum/u4l1a.cfm. Accessed 22 May 2023.
33   https://hbr.org/2009/06/rethinking-trust.
34   https://www.cairn.info/revue-economique-2017-5-page-859.htm.
35   IBID.
36   Meyer, Pamela. Liespotting: Proven Techniques to Detect Deception (p. 31). St. Martin's Press. Kindle Edition.
37   "MBTI® Basics." The Myers & Briggs Foundation, www.myersbriggs.org/my-mbti-personality-type/mbti-basics/. Accessed 26 May 2023.
38   Owens, Molly, and Christa Hardin. "What Is the Enneagram of Personality?" Truity, 3 Feb. 2023, www.truity.com/enneagram/what-is-enneagram.
39   Feltman, Charles. Thin Book of Trust: An Essential Primer for Building Trust at Work. 2nd ed., Thin Book Pub Co, 2021.
40   Wignall, Nick. "7 Psychological Reasons You Don't Trust Yourself." Nick Wignall, 1 Aug. 2021, nickwignall.com/7-psychological-reasons-you-dont-trust-yourself/.
41   Botsman, Rachel. "How to Trust Yourself More." How to Trust Yourself More - by Rachel Botsman, 23 Jan. 2023, rachelbotsman.substack.com/p/how-to-trust-yourself-more.
42   IBID.
43   Brown, Brené. "Dare to Lead the Braving Inventory." Brené Brown, 19 May 2023, brenebrown.com/resources/the-braving-inventory/.

44   Botsman, Rachel. "How to Trust Yourself More." How to Trust Yourself More - by Rachel Botsman, 23 Jan. 2023, rachelbotsman.substack.com/p/how-to-trust-yourself-more.
45   Wignall, Nick. "7 Psychological Reasons You Don't Trust Yourself." Nick Wignall, 1 Aug. 2021, nickwignall.com/7-psychological-reasons-you-dont-trust-yourself/.
46   Botsman, Rachel. "How to Trust Yourself More." How to Trust Yourself More - by Rachel Botsman, 23 Jan. 2023, rachelbotsman.substack.com/p/how-to-trust-yourself-more.
47   Horsager, David. Trusted Leader: 8 Pillars That Drive Results. Berrett-Koehler Publishers, Inc., 2021.
48   IBID.
49   Zak, Paul J. "The Neuroscience of Trust." Harvard Business Review, 2017, hbr.org/2017/01/the-neuroscience-of-trust.
50   "PWC's 25th Annual Global CEO Survey." Edited by Suzanne Snowden, PWC, 2016, www.pwc.com/gx/en/ceo-survey/2022/main/content/downloads/25th_CEO_Survey.pdf.
51   Chat.openai.com.
52   IBID.
53   Carucci, Ron. "How to Actually Encourage Employee Accountability." Harvard Business Review, 23 Nov. 2020, hbr.org/2020/11/how-to-actually-encourage-employee-accountability. (Ron Carucci is co-founder and managing partner at Navalent, working with CEOs and executives pursuing transformational change. He is the bestselling author of eight books, including To Be Honest and Rising to Power. Connect with him on LinkedIn at RonCarucci, and download his free "How Honest is My Team?" assessment.).
54   IBID.
55   "Accountability (n.)." Etymology, www.etymonline.com/word/accountability. Accessed 27 May 2023.
56   Carucci, Ron. "How to Actually Encourage Employee Accountability." Harvard Business Review, 23 Nov. 2020, hbr.org/2020/11/how-to-actually-encourage-employee-accountability.
57   IBID.
58   IBID.
59   Conley, Randy. "Just OK Is Not OK When It Comes to Being Trustworthy." Leading with Trust: Dependability Archives, 13 Jan. 2019, leadingwithtrust.com/category/dependability.
60   IBID.
61   Zenger, Jack, and Joseph Folkman. "The 3 Elements of Trust." Harvard Business Review, 5 Feb. 2019, hbr.org/2019/02/the-3-elements-of-trust.
62   Mankins, Michael, and Eric Garton. "How Spotify Balances Employee Autonomy and Accountability." Harvard Business Review, 9 Feb. 2017, hbr.org/2017/02/how-spotify-balances-employee-autonomy-and-accountability.
63   Anthony, Scott D. "Grooming Leaders to Handle Ambiguity." Harvard Business Review, 6 July 2010, hbr.org/2010/07/grooming-leaders-to-handle-ambiguity.
64   IBID.
65   Patton, Justin. "5 Ways to Build Trust between Coworkers." Fast Company: Career Evolution, 7 Jan. 2023, www.fastcompany.com/90830536/5-barriers-to-break-in-order-to-build-trust-between-coworkers.
66   IBID.
67   IBID.
68   IBID.

ABOUT THE AUTHORS

Joseph R. Myers
CEO and Chief Narratologist at Narratology

Joseph R. Myers is an entrepreneur, speaker, writer, and owner of josephrmyers.com, a consulting firm that assists organizations and individuals promote and develop healthy community and trust relationships. Author of best-selling books *The Search to Belong* and *Organic Community*, Myers works with some of North America's leading and most innovative organizations and faith-based businesses to strategize and re-imagine how to develop trusting, successful communities that result in a trust culture that influences strong top- and bottom-line growth.

Kevin E. Baird
Chairman, Center for College & Career Readiness

Kevin E. Baird is a noted leader in accelerated literacy development and priority instructional practices for equitable teaching and learning. In his role as Chairman at the nonprofit Center for College & Career Readiness, Mr. Baird collaborates with education leaders across the United States and around the world to deliver classroom experiences that accelerate student literacy. He is currently engaged in research focused on the need for psychological safety and prosocial environments to enable learning.

Kevin's recent projects include the design of graduate level courses for teachers and administrators focused on trauma readiness and trauma response, alongside his most recent book *Whole: What Teachers Need to Help Students Thrive* (with Rex Miller and Bill Lathan, Wiley 2020). He is co-author of the National Implementation Pathway for College & Career Readiness, has worked with the National Science Foundation funded Survey of Enacted Curriculum, and is currently involved in the study of student engagement using neurobiological measurement.

Kevin's work in early literacy includes the integration of foundational literacy skills into digital platforms; the development of language-rich, cognitive complex classrooms; and the development of global early literacy programs using mother tongue texts.

Beyond degrees in Sociology, Anthropology, and Business, Baird is one of the world's first Accredited Learning Environment Planners. He is a recipient of the Beinecke National Scholarship, has served as a Wingspread Fellow, and has participated in the Secretary's Circle at Phi Beta Kappa. His family foundation is actively involved in the development of schools and teachers globally, most recently with the building of new facilities across Nepal in collaboration with ADWAN.

Dr. Jesus F. Jara
Superintendent of Schools
Clark County School District

Since 2018, Dr. Jesus F. Jara has served as superintendent of the Clark County School District (CCSD), the fifth-largest school district in the nation. With a lifelong passion for creating better opportunities for all children through education, Dr. Jara's passion for education stems from his childhood experiences. Having moved from Venezuela to Miami as an English language learner, Dr. Jara faced many obstacles and challenges as he acclimated to the United States. His teachers, who were compassionate, inclusive, and set high expectations for all students, were a critical factor in his success.

Dr. Jara has been serving public school students for over 20 years. He served as the deputy superintendent for Orange County Public Schools in Florida and the superintendent and chief operations officer in Monroe County Public Schools. He has also served as an executive director of the College Board's Florida Partnership, a bilingual biology teacher, coach, assistant principal, and principal. Currently, he serves on the Executive Committee of the Council of Great City Schools, is a board member of the Association of Latino Administrators and Superintendents (ALAS), and is President of the Nevada Association of School Superintendents (NASS).

Dr. Jara received his Doctorate in Education, Educational Policy, Leadership, and Administration and was recently named Superintendent of the Year for Nevada

For more information and to schedule speaking/consulting opportunities contact us at:

josephrmyers.com

or email

trustme@josephrmyers.com

THANK YOU!

UNCHAINED receives a portion of the proceeds from this book to support its heroic efforts in fighting human trafficking.

If you'd like additional information or would like to support UNCHAINED directly, please visit www.unchained-freedom.com.

UNCHAINED
A Freedom Alliance

MORE FROM ME @pub

Surviving the Storm is educational, enjoyable, and ultimately **kind.** A gentle introduction to the concept that we have agency in our recovery from trauma.

Ainsley Sevier
co-host of Post-Orthodoxy

Scan Me